The Trees: Selected Poems 1967–2004

EUGENIO MONTEJO was born in Caracas, Venezuela, in 1938. He is the author of numerous books of poetry: *Élegos* (1967), *Muerte y memoria* (1972), *Algunas palabras* (1976), *Terredad* (1979), *Trópico absoluto* (1982), *Alfabeto del mundo* (1986), *Adiós al siglo XX* (1992), *El azul de la tierra* (1997), *Partitura de la cigarra* (1999) and *Tiempo Transfigurado* (2001). He has also published two collections of essays: *La ventana oblicua* and *El taller blanco*. In 1998 Eugenio Montejo received Venezuela's National Prize for Literature.

PETER BOYLE is an Australian poet. His four collections of poetry are *Coming home from the world* (1994), *The Blue Cloud of Crying* (1997), *What the painter saw in our faces* (2001), and *Museum of Space* (2004). A selection of his translations of César Vallejo, *I am going to speak of hope*, was published by the Peruvian Consulate, Sydney in 1999. He lives in Sydney where he works as a teacher.

MIGUEL GOMES is Professor of Comparative Literature at the University of Connecticut-Storrs. He is an essayist and a short-story writer.

The Trees

SELECTED POEMS 1967–2004

EUGENIO MONTEJO

Translated from the Spanish by PETER BOYLE
Introduced by MIGUEL GOMES

SALT

CAMBRIDGE

PUBLISHED BY SALT PUBLISHING
PO Box 937, Great Wilbraham, Cambridge PDO CB1 5JX United Kingdom
PO Box 202, Applecross, Western Australia 6153

© Eugenio Montejo, 2004
Translation copyright © Peter Boyle, 2004
Introduction copyright © Miguel Gomes, 2004

First published 2004

Printed and bound in the United Kingdom by Lightning Source

Typeset in Swift 9.5 / 13

ISBN 1 84471 035 1 paperback

SP

1 3 5 7 9 8 6 4 2

a Aymara y Emilio

Contents

Acknowledgments

Several of these translations have appeared, often in earlier or different versions, in the following magazines: "The Statue of Pessoa" in *Boxkite*; "Orpheus" in *Cordite*; "The Trees", "Iceland", "Ithaca" and "The White Workshop" in *Heat*; "The Trees", "Güigüe 1918", "The rooster's song" and excerpts from "Fragments" in *Jubilat* (USA); "The earth turned to bring us closer", "Life", "Caracas" and "Earthdom" in *sacredcat.org* (USA); "Left Behind" in *Shearsman* (UK); "The Other", "My elders" and "Earthness" in *Southerly*; "My ancestors", "Transfigured Time" in *Three Candles* (USA).

"At one time I wrote that poetry is a melodious chess game we play in solitude with God, maybe because I believe it approximates to a certain type of prayer in its dialogue with the mysterious. The fact is that in our times it constitutes the only religion that is left for us, at least the only one we can place against the omnipresent religion of money. Nevertheless, in recognising its closeness to prayer it is necessary to make it clear I'm referring to a naked prayer, a monologue with nothing in common, very distant from the political ritual of churches. It's a matter of a prayer spoken to a God who only exists while the prayer lasts. The only prayer finally adequate to invent that portion of God which everyone denies daily . . . "

— EUGENIO MONTEJO

Eugenio Montejo's Earthdom

By Miguel Gomes

Eugenio Montejo has written some of the most memorable poetry ever published in Venezuela. Since the late 1960s, a large number of demanding readers have been drawn to his work. The reasons are to be found in both his own stylistic mastery and the peculiar configuration of the Hispanic lyric tradition of the second half of the twentieth century.

Following the decline of the avant-garde and the quick canonization of those authors who reacted against it (Pablo Neruda, Octavio Paz, and Jorge Luis Borges, among others), the poets who began their careers in the 1960s have usually taken one of two opposite paths in their attempts to renew the expressive repertoire of the Spanish language. Some have chosen an extreme pathos reminiscent of what César Vallejo imagined as the unbearable "sickness of God". Others have resorted to a purely cerebral approach, manifested sometimes as prosaism (the so-called "anti-poetry" and its "urban" or "colloquial" offshoots) and sometimes as sheer addiction to the epigram (and any other means of cultivating a hyper-intellectual attitude).

Montejo, however, has shown a third way: undoubtedly contemporary, but free of modern poses (including the most modern of them all – the postmodern); full of human insight, but making no concessions to mawkishness; calm and sober, but with none of the severity or solemnity so often associated with the masters. This exemplary lack of interest in being fashionable or respectable has earned him the praise of numerous critics, who often qualify him as a timeless poet.

Timelessness, though, does not mean avoidance of history or its concrete social configurations. In fact, Montejo's complete indifference to fashion may be linked to a certain kind of political behavior I would term "oppositional".[1] According to such a perspective, the best way to prevent poetry from becoming one more article in a market of intellectual goods is to dissociate it from any linear conception of time that might impose itself upon the creative process. Since capitalism depends on the irrepressible production of novelty, deferring any passion for newness constitutes, at least symbolically, a negation of the capitalist world view and, more specifically, its main instinct – consumerism.

Montejo's commitment to autonomy, though, should not be equated with that of the symbolist or avant-garde poets, since it does not long for a verbal domain completely free from the transience and fragility of human experience. As a Spanish critic has stated, Montejo "has opted for memory, and such an option attests to his lack of faith in progress. Progress has killed our dead; it has favored the future over them. When we read his poetry we succumb to the sensation of being reached by the past, which has become a hidden aspect of the present, something we must uncover in order to restitute both memory and immediacy to their original state of communion".[2] According to this view, there is nothing conservative in Montejo's poetry because its goal is not a mere return to the past. His dead do not control the living, but are fully reintegrated into their current experiences. The resurrection of the past never freezes the present; rather, it enriches our desires and perceptions, and, moreover, gives us a feeling of continuity otherwise constantly lost in the feverish cult of the future. Although Montejo does not oppose chronology, he certainly opposes its modern capitalist version, one that persists in defining today as an abolition of yesterday. Unlike many cultural objects available nowadays, his poetry does not accuse other literary efforts of having ominous expiration dates. It never reminds us of the overwhelming power of products to come.

The best example of Montejo's critique of such a desperate *Weltanschauung* is "At the End of Everything", a piece unique in the poet's work for its openly sardonic vein. The denunciation of the tireless jumping forward proposed by the modern mind becomes a sort of cyclical labyrinth that soon wears out any attempt to avoid contradiction:

Nothing will remain of anyone or anything
but time circling and circling through itself;
time alone, invention of an invention,
that was invented also by another invention,
that was invented also by another invention,
that was . . .

Non-modern continuity, on the other hand, presupposes a strengthening of the links between men and cosmic rhythms. Nature's cycles shape those "ancient rites and celebrations" to which Montejo's poetry returns, according to one of his most authoritative critics.[3] And nature's cycles are also replicated and honored in Montejo's tendency toward thematic repetition and subtle variation, a tight system of self-quotations or self-allusions wonderfully termed *menciones migratorias* ("migratory mentions") by another critic.[4] The poet's work makes repeated mention of birds, trees, insects, horses, seasons, and landscapes, all of which are different but the same, because repetition underscores the fundamental and surprisingly minimalist cohesion of the universe. The secret connection of one bird to another and of one bird to its tree or to its song escalates into the universal synthesis of nature and human beings. It is no wonder that countless cities, myths, and historical characters and facts – as well as language itself – all become interwoven in the fabric of this cosmic poetry (or, as Montejo chooses to call it, this "Alphabet of the World").

The poet's decision, from this point of view, is still political, because it precludes the chance of conceiving any "non-human" (and, therefore, any "non-social") entity. As soon as nature is reached by our feelings or ideas, it is also assimilated into a dialogue in which myth and personal memory unite – and in which the divide between "self" and "other" is erased. This is why Montejo needs to coin the neologism *terredad* ("earthdom" or "earthness"). The new term springs not from some avant-garde attempt to astonish the reader; it is, rather, the only way of expressing the poet's belief in a primordial and always necessary union between culture and anything material existing independently of human beings. *Terredad* evokes a deeply socialized understanding of space, which is irreducible to merely physical, biological or geographical terms. It reminds us that people cannot conceive of anything around them without immediately marking it with subjective expectations; that space, as Henri Lefebvre would put it, can be and has been produced because it is both an embodiment and a medium of social life.[5] This concept of space as something that is neither strictly psychological nor strictly physical (but that, by the same token, cannot be completely separated from either mind or matter) is termed "spatiality" by Edward Soja; it implies, among other things, the end of the dichotomy nature/history as well as the notion that nature is also "filled with politics and ideology."[6]

Some of Montejo's most emblematic poems deal with the exchange of such apparent opposites in the midst of the main reversal that his work illustrates: the transformation of traditional objects into subjects. Thus, a bird-poet transfers its own qualities to a "song" that becomes a tangible thing in the world – one that might easily be identified with the poem enunciating such a possibility:

The earthdom of a bird is its song,
what leaves its breast and returns to the world,
the echoes of an invisible choir
in a forest long dead.
Its earthdom is its dream of finding itself
among all those absent ones [. . .].
In the dimension of time it is not a bird
but a single ray in the night of its species,
an interminable hunting for life
that the song may endure.

Montejo's reconfiguration of object and subject also allows us to experience a de-centered status such as the one described in the poem "Earthdom". The lyrical subject partakes in the multiplicity of life by avoiding the "I" and by using impersonal forms of the verb. What is usually small or insignificant becomes the equal of what is usually large or significant because there is a new cosmic order that is more just and less oriented by hierarchies. It is a cosmology in which nothing is central – and nothing is peripheral:

[xx]

To be here on earth; no more distant than a tree,
no more inexplicable;
thin in autumn, laden in summer,
with what we are and are not, with shadow,
memory, longing, until the end
(if there is one) voice to voice,
from house to house [. . .]
each time dividing our common bread
in two, in three, in four,
without forgetting the share for the ant . . .

Martin Buber once suggested that the origin of human consciousness is the recognition of a taut relationship between space and individual. The notion of being human grows from realizing the existence of a rift between what we are and everything else, between a space that we are and a space that we are not; inside and outside relate as strict opposites. But there should be, after such a primal setting-at-a-distance, a new phase in the process of becoming conscious: the recovery of what we once banished from ourselves. To be human means not only to create distances, but also to attempt to cross them, to re-appropriate them through emotion and involvement. Humanity arises from the interplay of distancing and the urge to overcome detachment. The reconnection of inside and outside materializes in a dialectical tension that produces a humanized second-nature.[7] This is what Montejo, in his wisely transparent language, calls "earthdom."

Of course, there is more to his vision of spatiality than metaphysics. He is a poet, but also a Venezuelan or Latin American poet – which entails a very concrete set of social references. The oppositional direction of Montejo's writing, in fact, can be situated in a precise context. When his first books were published, in the 1960s and 70s, Venezuela was showing many signs of a vigorous capitalist spatiality: the decadence of feudal property relations and the strengthening of a proletariat freed from its former means of subsistence (a transformation already in progress since the 1920s, when the dictator Juan Vicente Gómez gave the North American oil industry the monopoly of extracting and commercializing national gas reserves); the uprootings caused by the new commodification of rural and urban land; the geographical concentration of both labor and industrial production in urban centers, with the concomitant disintegration of earlier forms of urban and rural life; and, last but not least, the divorce of residence and workplace. Moreover, by the end of the 1950s, but very noticeably during the 1970s, the country was undergoing a number of remark-able changes due to a favorable international oil market. A prodigal State was fueling the development of a democracy prone to boast about its material resources, a democracy whose demagoguery and nouveau-riche spirit hailed the national present as an uninterrupted path of endless progress.

It is hardly surprising that Montejo chose to speak of trees, birds, roosters, oxen, horses, forests, and cicadas – topics having little or nothing at all to do with the only political or material reality imagi-nable back then. Such a choice was, in effect, the poet's subtle way of manifesting his disapproval without falling into a pamphleteer's rhet-oric (or losing the equilibrium of someone attuned to a lucid and harmonic cosmos). "Venezuela is rolling, and it is rolling in cars and trucks made in Venezuela; Chrysler is rolling along in step with the progress of a great democratic nation" – to this kind of optimistic assertion coming from both transnational corporations and Venezuelan oligarchies Montejo replied by questioning the mean-ing of modern urban life through anti-advertisement pieces such as "Mural Written by the Wind":

Cities promise themselves to every new arrival
but love no one.
When seen through the windows of a plane
all of them draw you in
with their blue heights
and long noisy boulevards,
but with time they become bitter shadows.
Their buildings make us lonely,
their cemeteries are full of suicides
who didn't even leave behind a note.

Sometimes Montejo's approach is more indirect. His poems celebrate places imbued not with material opulence but with myth and poetical richness. "Iceland," for instance, maps the contradictions of an encounter between everyday life and the imagination. "Lisbon" evokes a city founded, according to ancient legends, by Ulysses. Montejo's own Venezuela is suddenly once again "Manoa", the capital of the golden kingdom sought by the Conquistadors.

The rural world is also central in this poetry, and for the same reasons. The remembrance of a provincial youth or of a now-remote original land of ancestors (see "My Ancestors" or "Güigüe 1918") offers multiple opportunities to reassert the basic advantages that a realm of emotions and deeply rooted feelings has over a "rolling nation" full of contempt for the past. In some poems, and even in the lyrical atmosphere of his essays, Montejo's reminiscence of his father, Eduardo, who had a bakery (a "white workshop"), opens a venue for recreating a space that is "other" but still possible. It is real because, contrary to utopias, it exists in our conscience, in our memory, and in certain private portions of our awareness of what we are.

By the end of the 1980s the apparent prosperity of the petroleum-rich Venezuela faded away like a mirage. As continuous devaluations of the currency took the middle and lower classes by surprise, their consumer habits had to change. Disenchantment and anger were the prevalent attitudes in the new era. The 1990s and the beginning of the 2000s have been marked by the obvious dismantling of the demagoguery of progress and the unexpected return of an older form of demagoguery, one rooted in the semi-feudal Venezuela of the nineteenth century and its cult of military heroes. Although superficially refurbished with eye-catching and ear-pleasing "revolutionary" imagery, the current Venezuelan *neocaudillismo* (that is, the adoration of a strong ruler with a highly individualized and egocentric leadership style) imposes upon the present a cult of the past. But this past, instead of the spiritual environment often recreated by Montejo's poetry, has proven to be a solemn and archaic idolization of founding fathers with no positive effect whatsoever on the country, now officially renamed *República Bolivariana de Venezuela*. The "Bolivarian Republic" created by Hugo Chávez's regime in 1998 amounts to a new mirage, a grotesque cover-up for an undoubtedly reactionary revival of old ghosts. This is the past that Montejo's poetry abhors:

The same sun-washed countryside remains,
untamed landscapes, fast music,
mines, wide plains, petroleum,
this land of ours flowing in our veins
that's never managed to bury Gómez.

"A Photograph from 1948," from which the above excerpt is taken, is one of the few poems that make specific references to the country's history. Juan Vicente Gómez, the old dictator of a backward land, seems to be alive after so many years; long forgotten problems and tribulations, despite all the promises of change, are suddenly seen to have survived.

We should remember, however, that nature and culture are both part of the same reality. Wide plains, music, and petroleum intermingle chaotically and coexist in a land "flowing in our veins" that is not necessarily doomed; since nature has a way of renewing itself, the reader could surmise that hope is also available for people's deeds. In fact, Montejo's tone, even in the worst circumstances, sings to calmness and peaceful harmony. Such is the score of his cicada and, undoubtedly, his own, because tomorrow "there will be other voices on earth" and the cicada "is dreaming in our blood."

Notes

1 In the sense Edward Said uses the word. See *The World, the Text, and the Critic*, Cambridge, Mass.: Harvard UP, 1983, p. 29.

2 Francisco José Cruz Pérez, "Eugenio Montejo: el viaje total" in *Eugenio Montejo, Antología*, Caracas: Monte Ávila Editores, 1996, p. 8.

3 Francisco Rivera, "La poesía de Eugenio Montejo", *Inscripciones*, Caracas: Fundarte, 1982, p.90.

4 Pedro Lastra, "El pan y las palabras: poesía de Eugenio Montejo" in Pedro Lastra and Luis Eyzaguirre, eds. *Catorce poetas hispanoamericanos de hoy*, special issue of *Inti* 18–9 (1984), Rhode Island, U.S.A, p.213.

5 Henri Lefebvre, *La Production de l'espace*, Paris: Anthropos, 1974.

6 Edward Soja, *Postmodern Geographies: The Reassertion of Space in Critical Social Theory*, London/New York: Verso, 1989, p. 121.

7 Martin Buber, "Distance and Relation", *Psychiatry* 20 (1957): pp. 97–104.

Translator's Preface

It has been both a great joy and a great responsibility to have worked for some six years now on translating the poetry of Eugenio Montejo. To discover a great poet is always something joyful. On the other hand, knowing how little of Montejo's poetry has been translated into English, I have felt a very strong responsibility to remain as close as possible to the meaning and spirit of the original. Of course literal fidelity is not always the most important form of fidelity and, as a poet, I have been equally concerned with the other dimensions of sound, imagery, pacing, and (perhaps above all) tone.

Responsibility for the choice of poems presented here is also my own. The poems translated come from the collections *El azul de la tierra* (Bogotá, 1997), *Adiós al siglo XX* (Sevilla, 1997), *Tiempo Transfigurado* (Valencia, Venezuela, 2001) and *Partitura de la cigarra* (Madrid, 1999), apart from two earlier poems: "Caracas" from *Terredad* and "La tierra giró para acercarnos" from the Mexican edition of *Alfabeto del Mundo*. However, these four later collections themselves gather poems written over Montejo's entire career as a poet, from the 1960s through to the close of the last century. I have made no attempt to reproduce a chronological order – something Montejo himself does not do in his collections, preferring to let each poem greet the reader as if it was written in the same time frame. In this way, the ordering can set up resonances and echoes, whilst maintaining variety for the reader.

In making my selection I was guided initially by what I felt most drawn to as a poet and what seemed to go over most successfully into English. Over time I have added poems like "Elegía a la muerte de mi hermano Ricardo" and the excerpt from "Partitura de la cigarra", poems which, despite the many difficulties in tone and balance they present to an English translator, seem essential to any just appraisal of Montejo's work. There have also been late finds, poems which I overlooked for a long time but which in the final months of preparing this book impressed me with their resonant imagery, emotional force and subtlety of tone. Among such poems are "En el Café", "Final de lluvia" and "Medianoche".

I first met Eugenio Montejo at the poetry festival in Medellín, Colombia, in 1997. Reading with growing absorption his collection "El azul de la tierra" I made my first attempts to translate the poems "Islandia" and "Los árboles". What impressed me immediately with Montejo's poetry was its moral authority, its emotional depth, the humanity and humility it displayed, along with great poetic subtlety and beauty. The attractions of Montejo's poetry are many. Perhaps the key attraction is that his poetry is so authentic and open. It addresses without shame the experiences of ageing, of loss, of disappointment, as of disinterested love, of the simple joys of living, the early morning coffee and the stars at night. Poetically-speaking Eugenio Montejo's poetry creates for itself a space very difficult to find in late twentieth century English-language poetry: it borders on the romanticism of a Yeats or Wordsworth yet it is distinctly modern. Often marked by irony and disillusionment, it speaks of an immense faith in the beauty and unity of life. Montejo manages to sidestep fashions and poses to get down to what in his prose piece "Fragments" he terms "the emotional nakedness of the world".

Subtle modulations of tone seem to me all important in this poetry – as if, whilst being entirely natural and unselfconscious, the poet is also walking a tightrope between a lush romanticism and a bald matter-of-factness. This can be sensed in the rhythm of the language itself. To consider the Spanish of "Los árboles" ("The Trees"):

> Hablan poco los árboles, se sabe.
> Pasan la vida entera meditando
> y moviendo sus ramas.
> Basta mirarlos en otoño
> cuando se juntan en los parques:
> sólo conversan los más viejos (. . .)

The opening line is a kind of matter-of-fact intimate speech heightened just slightly by the inversion of the word order but then brought to earth by the edge of colloquialism in "se sabe". The next two lines stretch wide in their rapture – "la vida entera" and that wonderfully mimetic word "meditando". "Basta miralos en otoño" continues this delicate off-play between everydayness and an edge of lifting picked up first in the voice. The perils of translating this into English can be seen if we said: "It's enough to look at them in autumn/when they join together in parks:/only the oldest converse . . ." Translated in this way, a dull flatness has replaced the limpid tension of Montejo's Spanish. An astute reader may well notice that I often have more words than are there in the original. One factor influencing this is rhythm. Polysyllabic Spanish words can produce an abrupt flatness when replaced by monosyllabic English words. That edge of lushness, of a wider rhythm, seems to me an important dimension in Montejo's poetry, even though it is often held in check by irony and colloquialism. Another factor that has led me to add slightly here or there is the need to match shifts in tone and attitude, to put back into the English poem something lost as we go into the sometimes one-dimensional world of English. For me the major consideration has been that these poems start as engaging, forceful poems in Spanish and, if the translation is to be worth anything at all, must end up as poems that work in their new-found language.

Montejo's poetry is strongly marked by his concise, elegant, slightly elliptical use of language. Part of the difficulty in translating his poetry arises from the way words in the two languages occupy different spaces. Often in Spanish the one word has both a formal and an everyday usage, whereas English has two distinctive words. A poet like Montejo gains brevity and force by skillfully using words that are formal and elegant yet steeped in a lived reality, neither abstract nor narrowly colloquial. "Adiós" is both "farewell" and the familiar "goodbye". "Fiesta" can be a party, a festival, a celebration, perhaps a carnival, and of course a fiesta. English requires us to choose one of these words, fixing ourselves more narrowly. Likewise to give a spoken "feel" to English it is often necessary to add more words – the small qualifiers we use to build in attitude. Simplicity is also helped by the rich music of the Spanish language. Often sound alone achieves in Montejo's poetry what requires an added word or image in the English. When in the poem "Caracas" Montejo describes ibis feathers as "egipcias claridades" he doesn't need to use the word "soft", the sounds do that already. Even when the dictionary seems to affirm identity, like the Spanish "tatuados" and the English "tattooed", much of the Spanish word's poetic force in a poem like *Adiós al siglo XX* lies in its richness as an open-voweled, four syllable word. Thus, to translate "pequeños guijarros/ tatuados de rumor infinito" I opted for "small pebbles/ chipped and rounded by infinite echoes", as a closer match in syllables and sounds, giving a better sense of the tactile feel of the original.

Working on translations, I am conscious I am moving not just between two languages but between two different poetic traditions with their own distinctive ways of giving a poem "lift off" and of conveying emotions. In Spanish (as in French and Greek) the rich sounds of the language create an oral texture that tends to favour a direct naming of familiar objects, feelings and experiences, whereas within English-language-poetry unusual images and metaphors can seem almost *de rigeur*. Writers of poetry in English battle with a century of our language being the international language of kitsch, of pop songs, of advertisements, of the degradation of words like "truth", "love", "pain", but equally words like "candle", "fire", "moon", "stars". Likewise English-language poetry since the close of the nineteenth century has favoured the earthing of all emotions in the detailed description of events or realities. A comparison of Montejo's poems dealing with his father or the loss of his brother with, for example, Sharon Olds' poems about her father in *The Dead and the Living* or Philip Levine's moving portraits of his family in *The Simple Truth* reveals the divide between Hispanic and Anglo-saxon poetic traditions. Such a comparison is not to devalue either side but merely to highlight different cultural assumptions about how poetry best speaks the truth about our lives.

Part of the charm and power of Montejo's poetry comes from the simplicity of his building blocks – both the words and images, and the syntax and poetic devices used. Consider the poem "Medianoche":

Escribo tarde. Es medianoche.
Ignoro cuándo he remontado este camino,
cómo llegué donde me encuentro, qué buscaba.

The plainness of the opening, the next two lines unobtrusively shifting the viewpoint from one evening to a lifetime, the slightly elliptical feel of the Spanish, the heightened tone of "*me encuentro*" ("I find myself/ I am") – all locate us in a deeply-lived reality, reached directly without the encasement of biographic detail. The poem then shifts to an image, the most obvious stellar image, the Southern Cross, in "*la radiante soledad nocturna*": "the radiant (or shining or bright) nocturnal loneliness or solitude". This last phrase exemplifies a dilemma frequently facing the translator. How to translate a word like "*soledad*", with its varying meanings of aloneness, solitude and loneliness? At this point the poem's protagonist is able to speak to us directly in an immediate personal voice: "*No estoy seguro aquí de nada*" (I'm not sure here of anything). The poem closes with one of Montejo's favourite familiars, the roosters. Beyond Esculapius, Socrates and Christ appears the image of the poet's father, scattering their cries "like crumbs of lightning". This thirteen line poem with its sparse, almost minimal vocabulary and few images, manages to summon in a deeply authentic way both the quest for human goodness and the scepticism befitting most of its worldly, intellectual expositions.

Among the many personal favourites collected here, I would like to conclude with two examples of the authenticity and dignity I sense in Montejo's voice as a poet. "El rezagado" ("Left Behind") confronts death in a way both ancient and modern. Planes crossing the sky and shady suburban streets are as at home here as ghosts and the monologues of clouds. The dream, a common one perhaps, of witnessing one's own funeral, is here lived through with a waking clear-sightedness that involves both all the skills of a poet and fidelity to the unspoken weight of being human. In a lighter vein is the poem "En el Café" ("In the Café"). What at first looks like a lament for ageing, for the transition from youth to mid-life, becomes instead, through the ambivalent image of rain, a wonderful reflection on the value of art. Such a summary, of course, passes over the poem's great humour and delicacy of tone.

By coincidence, one Wednesday night in 1997 in Medellín – I have remembered this only recently – I was fortunate enough to hear Montejo read both "El rezagado" and "En el Café" – a measured clear reading to a crowded hall filled with people accustomed to grasping in a recital of poetry both its artistic shape and its emotional power. My head, at that time reeling from so much Spanish and shutting down from the effort required for me to follow it all, took in only so much of the precise words – but the rhythm of the voice and the feel of what passed between poet and audience remain clear with me. If poetry is about speaking authentically of what genuinely matters, Eugenio Montejo's poetry certainly does that.

In preparing these translations I have been helped by many people. It was the Colombian poet and friend Guillermo Martínez who at the Medellín festival first suggested I pay close attention to Montejo's poetry as something very special I was sure to respond to. Mario Licón Cabrera and Juan Garrido Salgado have helped out on several occasions by reviewing my versions, providing that most fruitful thing for a translator, the responses of a native speaker of the language. Martin Harrison discussed early versions of these translations with me, making me more aware of the strongly oral quality of Montejo's verse. Judith Beveridge kindly read through the translations, making valuable suggestions on my wording in "The cicada's score". I owe thanks to Margie Cronin for listening patiently to my discussion of several poems where the choice between alternative versions had me confused. In the last phase of preparing this book for publication I have been greatly assisted by the generous advice of Jordi Doce who queried various places where I had strayed from Montejo's literal meaning. Someone who has been of great assistance over the years, helping with unknown words or passages unclear to me, is Miguel Gomes. I am also deeply indebted to Miguel for his scholarly and insightful Introduction, as well as for preparing the bibliography.

The most important friend and assistant in the preparation of this book is, of course, Eugenio Montejo himself. Over many years through letters and emails, Eugenio Montejo has tirelessly answered queries, made suggestions about the meanings of words and phrases, explained personal or local references, and steered me in the way of friends and materials that might help me in my task of understanding his work. Both for his sincere friendship and for the depth and beauty of his work, I count myself very privileged to have encountered the poetry of Eugenio Montejo.

PETER BOYLE

The Trees: Selected Poems (1967–2004)

Los Árboles

Hablan poco los árboles, se sabe.
Pasan la vida entera meditando
y moviendo sus ramas.
Basta mirarlos en otoño
cuando se juntan en los parques:
sólo conversan los más viejos,
los que reparten las nubes y los pájaros,
pero su voz se pierde entre las hojas
y muy poco nos llega, casi nada.

Es difícil llenar un breve libro
con pensamientos de árboles.
Todo en ellos es vago, fragmentario.
Hoy, por ejemplo, al escuchar el grito
de un tordo negro, ya en camino a casa,
grito final de quien no aguarda otro verano,
comprendí que en su voz hablaba un árbol,
uno de tantos,
pero no sé qué hacer con ese grito,
no sé cómo anotarlo.

The Trees

The trees speak so little, you know.
They spend their entire life meditating
and moving their branches.
Just look at them closely in autumn
as they seek each other out in public places:
only the oldest attempt some conversation,
the ones that share clouds and birds,
but their voice gets lost in the leaves
and so little filters down to us, nothing really.

It's difficult to fill the shortest book
with the thoughts of trees.
Everything in them is vague, fragmented.
Today, for instance, on the way to my house
hearing a black thrush shriek,
the last cry of one who won't reach another summer,
I realized that in his voice a tree was speaking,
one of so many,
but I don't know what to do with this sharp deep sound,
I don't know in what type of script
I could set it down.

Islandia

Islandia y lo lejos que nos queda,
con sus brumas heladas y sus fiordos
donde se hablan dialectos de hielo.

Islandia tan próxima del polo,
purificada por las noches
en que amamantan las ballenas.

Islandia dibujada en mi cuaderno,
la ilusión y la pena (o viceversa).

¿Habrá algo más fatal que este deseo
de irme a Islandia y recitar sus sagas,
de recorrer sus nieblas?

Es este sol de mi país
que tanto quema
el que me hace soñar con sus inviernos.
Esta contradicción ecuatorial
de buscar una nieve
que preserve en el fondo su calor,
que no borre las hojas de los cedros.

Nunca iré a Islandia. Está muy lejos.
A muchos grados bajo cero.
Voy a plegar el mapa para acercarla.
Voy a cubrir sus fiordos con bosques de palmeras.

Iceland

Iceland and the distances which are left us,
with their frozen mists and fjords
where they speak dialects of ice.

Iceland so close to the pole,
purified by nights
where the whales suckle their young.

Iceland drawn in my exercise book,
the illusion and the tragedy (or vice-versa).

Could anything be more ill-fated than this longing
to go to Iceland and recite its sagas,
to traverse its fogs?

It's the sun of my country
which burns so much
that makes me dream of its winters.
This equatorial contradiction
of seeking a snow that preserves heat at its core,
that doesn't strip the cedars of their leaves.

I will never get to Iceland. It's very far.
Many degrees below zero.
I'm going to fold the map over and bring Iceland closer.
I'm going to cover its fjords with palm tree groves.

Güigüe 1918

a Juan Liscano

Ésta es la tierra de los míos, que duermen, que no duermen,
largo valle de cañas frente a un lago,
con campanas cubiertas de siglos y polvo
que repiten de noche los gallos fantasmas.
Estoy a veinte años de mi vida,
no voy a nacer ahora que hay peste en el pueblo,
las carretas se cargan de cuerpos y parten;
son pocas las zanjas abiertas;
las campanas cansadas de doblar
bajan y cavan.
Puedo aguardar, voy a nacer muy lejos de este lago,
de sus miasmas;
mi padre partirá con los que queden,
lo esperaré más adelante.
Ahora soy esta luz que duerme, que no duerme;
atisbo por el hueco de los muros;
los caballos se atascan en fango y prosiguen;
miro la tinta que anota los nombres,
la caligrafía salvaje que imita los pastos.
La peste pasará. Los libros en el tiempo amarillo
seguirán tras las hojas de los árboles.
Palpo el temblor de llamas en las velas
cuando las procesiones recorren las calles.
No he de nacer aquí,
hay cruces de zábila en las puertas
que no quieren que nazca;
queda mucho dolor en las casas de barro.
Puedo aguardar, estoy a veinte años de mi vida,
soy el futuro que duerme, que no duerme;
la peste me privará de voces que son mías,
tendré que reinventar cada ademán, cada palabra.

Güigüe 1918

to Juan Liscano

This is the land of my people who sleep, who don't sleep,
wide valley of cane fields opposite a lake,
and church bells mired with centuries of dust
that ghostly roosters echo through the night.
I am twenty years ahead of my own life,
I will not be born now since there is plague in the village,
carts laden with corpses move off;
there are few ditches left open;
the bells tired of tolling for the dead
are brought down and lowered deep in wells.
I can wait,
I will be born very far from this lake and its miasmas;
my father will set off with those who are left,
I will wait for him further on.
Now I am the light which sleeps, which does not sleep;
I can see it through the hollow of the walls.
Horses bogged in mud keep struggling forwards;
I can see the ink that copies people's names,
the wild calligraphy that mimics abandoned fields.
The plague will pass. Books in that yellow time
will imitate the leaves of trees.
I can touch the candle flames as they tremble
in processions passing by along the streets.
I am not going to be born here,
chalk crosses mark the doors
of those who don't want me to be born;
there is deep pain in the mud-brick houses.
I can wait; I am twenty years ahead of my own life,
I'm the future that sleeps, that doesn't sleep.
The plague robs me of voices that are mine;
I shall have to reinvent every gesture, each word.

Ahora soy esta luz al fondo de sus ojos;
ya naceré después, llevo escrita mi fecha;
estoy aquí con ellos hasta que se despidan;
sin que puedan mirarme me detengo:
quiero cerrarles suavemente los párpados.

Now I am that light in the depths of his eyes;
I will be born later on, the date is already written.
I stay here with them as they say their farewells;
although they can't see me I remain in their presence;
I would like so softly to close their eyelids for them.

El Canto del Gallo

a Adriano González León

El canto está fuera del gallo;
está cayendo gota a gota entre su cuerpo,
ahora que duerme en el árbol.
Bajo la noche cae, no cesa de caer
desde la sombra entre sus venas y sus alas.
El canto está llenando, incontenible,
al gallo como un cántaro;
llena sus plumas, su cresta, sus espuelas,
hasta que lo desborda y suena inmenso el grito
que a lo largo del mundo sin tregua se derrama.
Después el aleteo retorna a su reposo
y el silencio se vuelve compacto.
El canto de nuevo queda fuera
esparcido a la sombra del aire.
Dentro del gallo sólo hay vísceras y sueño
y una gota que cae en la noche profunda,
silenciosamente, al tic-tac de los astros.

The Rooster's Song

to Adriano González León

The song is there outside the rooster;
it's falling drop by drop inside his body
now he is sleeping in the tree.
All through the night it falls, does not stop falling
from the darkness between his veins and wings.
Uncontainable, the song fills the rooster
like a deep pitcher;
it fills his feathers, his crest, his spurs
until its enormous cry breaks the limit of his being
and rings out,
spilling without pause down the length of the world.
After that the rooster's breathing rests
and silence pulses, tense, solid.
Once again the song is outside
scattered in the black wind.
Inside the rooster there is only entrails and sleep
and a small drop that falls in the depths of night
silently to the tic-tac of stars.

Within all
of us...

[11]

La Estatua de Pessoa

a Rafael Cadenas

La estatua de Pessoa nos pesa mucho,
hay que llevarla despacio.
Descansemos un poco aquí a la vuelta
mientras vienen más gentes en ayuda.
Tenemos tiempo de tomar un trago.

Son tantas sombras en un mismo cuerpo
y debemos subirlas a la cumbre del Chiado.
A cada paso se intercambian idiomas,
anteojos, sombreros, soledades.

Démosle vino ahora. Pessoa siempre bebía
en estos bares de borrosos espejos
que el Tajo cruza en un tranvía sonámbulo.
¿Por qué no va a beber su estatua?

Con todo el siglo dentro de sus huesos
vueltos ya piedras llenas de saudades,
casi nos dobla los hombros
bajo el silencio de su risa pagana.

No hay que apurarse. Llegaremos.
Lo que más cuesta no es la altura de su cuerpo
ni el largo abrigo que lo envuelve,
sino las horas del misterio
que se repliegan pétreas en el mármol.
Cuanto a diario soñó por estas calles
y desoñó y volvió a soñar y desoñar;
el tiempo refractado en voces y antivoces
y los horóscopos oscuros
que lo han cubierto como una gruesa pátina.
Alzar sólo su cuerpo sería fácil.
Aunque se embriague no pesa más que un pájaro.

The Statue of Pessoa

to Rafael Cadenas

The statue of Pessoa weighs heavily on our shoulders.
We have to carry it slowly.
Let's rest here a little at the corner
while more people can come out and help.
We've got time for a quick drink.

There are so many darknesses in a single body
and we have to carry them up to the summit of Chiado.
At each step languages are exchanged,
glasses, hats, lonelinesses.

Let's share a wine with him now. Pessoa always drank
in these bars of clouded mirrors
crossing the Tagus in a sleepwalking streetcar.
Why shouldn't his statue stop for a drink?

With the whole century in his bones
now turned to stones filled with nostalgias,
our shoulders almost buckle
under the silence of his pagan laughter.

There's no need to hurry. We'll get there.
The tough thing isn't the height of his body
or the wide coat which covers it
but the hours of mystery
folded over and over petrified in the marble.
How many times each day
did he dream in these streets
and undream and go back to dreaming and undreaming;
time fractured in voices and opposing voices,
the dark horoscopes
that covered him like a thick patina.
To lift only his body would be easy.
High, intoxicated,
it weighs no more than a bird.

Sobremesa

A tientas, al fondo de la niebla
que cae de los remotos días,
volvemos a sentarnos
y hablamos ya sin vernos.
A tientas, al fondo de la niebla.

Sobre la mesa vuelve el aire
y el sueño atrae a los ausentes.
Panes donde invernaron musgos fríos
en el mantel ahora se despiertan.

Yerran vapores de café
y en el aroma, reavivados,
vemos flotar antiguos rostros
que empañan los espejos.

Rectas sillas vacías
aguardan a quienes, desde lejos,
retornarán más tarde.
Comenzamos a hablar
sin vernos y sin tiempo.

A tientas, en la vaharada
que crece y nos envuelve,
charlamos horas sin saber
quién vive todavía, quién está muerto.

Talking Across the Table

Hesitantly, surrounded
by the mist that falls from days long gone,
we once more sit down to talk
and can't see each other.
Hesitantly, cut off in the depths of the mist.

On the table the breeze stirs slowly.
As we dream those who are absent draw close.
Loaves where bleak moss has passed long winters
now waken on the table-cloth.

Steam from the coffee cups drifts around us
and in the aroma we see old faces,
once more alive, float past
clouding the mirrors.

Empty chairs set straight
wait for those who, from far off,
will return later on.
We start talking
without seeing each other, without thought of time.

Hesitantly, in the mist
that grows and surround us,
we talk for hours without knowing
who is still alive and who is dead.

Ítaca

Para un homenaje a C. Cavafy

Por esta calle se va a Ítaca
y en su rumor de voces, pasos, sombras,
cualquier hombre es Ulises.
Grabado entre sus piedras se halla el mapa
de esa tierra añorada. Síguelo.
El pájaro que escuchas está cantando en griego;
no lo traduzcas, no va a ahorrarte camino.
Aquellas nubes vienen de su mar, contémplalas;
son más puros los cielos de las islas.
Por esta calle, en cualquier auto,
hacia el norte o el sur se viaja a Ítaca.
En los ojos de los paseantes arde su fuego;
sus pasos rápidos delatan el exilio.
Aun sin moverte, como estos árboles,
hoy o mañana llegarás a Ítaca.
Está escrita en la palma de tu mano
como una raya que se ahonda
día tras día.
Aunque te duermas despertarás en Ítaca;
la lluvia de este valle todo lo arrastra
despacio hasta sus puertas.
No tiene otro declive.
Ya puedes anunciarnos tu llegada, buscar hotel,
dar al olvido tu destierro.
Por esta calle no ha cruzado un hombre
que al fin no alcance su paisaje.
Prepara el corazón para el arribo.
Una vez en su reino, muestra tu magia,
será el reto supremo del exilio.
A ese mar no se miente. La furia de sus olas
todo lo hace naufragio. Pero no te amilanes.
Demuéstranos que siempre fuiste Ulises.

Ithaca

by way of homage to C. Cavafy

On this street you go to Ithaca
and in its medley of voices, footsteps, shadows,
every man is Ulysses.
Engraved on its stones you will find
the map of this longed-for land.
Follow it.
The bird you hear is singing in Greek.
Don't translate it; it's not going to shorten your journey.
Those clouds come from its sea; contemplate them –
even purer are the skies of its islands.
On this road, in whatever car,
travelling north or south, you are travelling to Ithaca.
In the eyes of passers-by burns its fire.
The speed of their steps betrays exile.
Even without moving, like these trees,
today or tomorrow you will arrive at Ithaca.
It is written in the palm of your hand
like a line that deepens
day after day.
Even though you fall asleep you will awake in Ithaca;
the rain of this valley will slowly strip away
everything right up to the gates of Ithaca.
There is no other slope to the land.
Now you can announce your arrival,
find a hotel, give to oblivion your time of exile.
No man has crossed this street
who hasn't finally achieved his own landscape.
Make your heart ready for the moment of arrival.
Once in its kingdom, reveal your magic;
it will be the supreme challenge of exile.
On this sea there are no lies. The fury of its waves
overturns all boats. But don't be scared.
Show to us that you were always Ulysses.

La Terredad de un Pájaro

La terredad de un pájaro es su canto,
lo que en su pecho vuelve al mundo
con los ecos de un coro invisible
desde un bosque ya muerto.
Su terredad es el sueño de encontrarse
en los ausentes,
de repetir hasta el final la melodía
mientras crucen abiertas los aires
sus alas pasajeras;
aunque no sepa a quién le canta
ni por qué,
ni si podrá escucharse en otros algún día
como cada minuto quiso ser:
—más inocente.
Desde que nace nada ya lo aparta
de su deber terrestre;
trabaja al sol, procrea, busca sus migas
y es sólo su voz lo que defiende,
porque en el tiempo no es un pájaro
sino un rayo en la noche de su especie,
una persecución sin tregua de la vida
para que el canto permanezca.

The Earthdom of a Bird

The earthdom of a bird is its song,
what leaves its breast and returns to the world,
the echoes of an invisible choir
in a forest long dead.
Its earthdom is the dream of finding itself
among all those absent ones,
of repeating the melody right to the end
while its travelling wings cross
the open breezes;
even though it doesn't know for whom it sings
or why
or if one day it will be able to hear itself in others
as every minute it would like to be:
more innocent.
From birth nothing separates it
from its earthly task;
it toils in the sun, procreates, looks for crumbs
and only its voice defends it
for in the dimension of time it is not a bird
but a single ray in the night of its species,
an interminable hunting for life
that the song may endure.

Caracas

Tan altos son los edificios
que ya no se ve nada de mi infancia.
Perdí mi patio con sus lentas nubes
donde la luz dejó plumas de ibis,
egipcias claridades;
perdí mi nombre y el sueño de mi casa.
Rectos andamios, torre sobre torre,
nos ocultan ahora la montaña.
El ruido crece a mil motores por oído,
a mil autos por pie, todos mortales.
Los hombres corren detrás de sus voces
pero las voces van a la deriva
detrás de los taxis.
Más lejana que Tebas, Troya, Nínive
y los fragmentos de sus sueños,
Caracas, ¿dónde estuvo?
Perdí mi sombra y el tacto de sus piedras,
ya no se ve nada de mi infancia.
Puedo pasearme ahora por sus calles
a tientas, cada vez más solitario;
su espacio es real, impávido, concreto,
sólo mi historia es falsa.

Caracas

The buildings are so high
nothing can be seen now of my childhood.
I've lost my patio with its lazy clouds
where the light dropped ibis feathers,
soft Egyptian clarities.
I've lost my name and the dream of my house.
Rigid frames of buildings, tower on tower,
now hide the mountain from us.
The racket grows with a thousand motorcars for each ear,
a thousand sets of wheels for each foot, all of them deadly.
Men race after their voices
but their voices have wandered off
chasing the taxis.
More distant than Thebes, Troy, Nineveh
or the fragments of their dreams,
Caracas, where are you?
I've lost my own shadow and the feel of its stones.
Nothing can be seen any more of my childhood.
I stroll through its streets now
like a blind man, each day more solitary.
Its space is real, fearless, solid concrete.
Only my history is false.

Mis Mayores

a Alberto Patiño

Mis mayores me dieron la voz verde
y el límpido silencio que se esparce
allá en los pastos del lago Tacarigua.
Ellos van a caballo por las haciendas.
Hace calor. Yo soy el horizonte
de ese paisaje adonde se encaminan.

Oigo los sones de sus roncas guitarras
cuando cruzan el polvo y recorren mi sangre
a través de un amargo perfume de jobos.
Bajo mi carne se ven unos a otros
tan nítidos que puedo contemplarlos.
Y si hablo solo, son ellos quienes hablan
en las gavillas de sus cañamelares.
Hace calor. Yo soy el muro tenso
donde está fija su hilera de retratos.

Mis mayores van y vienen por mi cuerpo,
son un aire sin aire que sopla del lago,
un galope de sombras que desciende
y se borra en lejanas sementeras.
Por donde voy llevo la forma del vacío
que los reúne en otro espacio, en otro tiempo.
Hace calor. Hace el verde calor que en mí los junta.
Yo soy el campo donde están enterrados.

My Ancestors

to Alberto Patiño

My ancestors gave me the green voice
and limpid silences that spread
there in the grasslands around Lake Tacarigua.
They travel on horseback around the haciendas.
It's hot. I am the horizon of this landscape
where they are heading.

In the bitter fragrance of the joba trees
I hear the sounds of their harsh guitars
crossing the dust and traversing my blood.
Under my skin they look at each other
so sharply I can almost see their faces.
And when I talk to myself, they are the ones speaking
in the rustling sheaves of the sugar plantations.
It's hot. I am the tense wall
where their portraits hang in a row.

My ancestors come and go through my body,
with the airless breeze sighing from the lake,
the galloping of dark shapes that come down
to be lost among distant seedtimes.
Wherever I go I carry the shape of emptiness
that unites them all in a different space, a different time.
It's hot. It's the green heat that joins them to me.
I am the fields where they are buried.

Mi Amor

En otro cuerpo va mi amor por esta calle,
siento sus pasos debajo de la lluvia,
caminando, soñando, como en mí hace ya tiempo...
Hay ecos de mi voz en sus susurros,
puedo reconocerlos.
Tiene ahora una edad que era la mía,
una lámpara que siempre se enciende al encontrarnos.
Mi amor que se embellece con el mal de las horas,
mi amor en la terraza de un Café
con un hibisco blanco entre las manos,
vestida a la usanza del nuevo milenio.
Mi amor que seguirá cuando me vaya,
con otra risa y otros ojos,
como una llama que dio un salto entre dos velas
y se quedó alumbrando el azul de la tierra.

My Love

In another body my love moves along this street.
I hear her footsteps under the rain,
walking, dreaming, as I did years ago . . .
There are echoes of my voice in her whispered sighs,
I recognise them.
She is now the same age that I was then,
a light that's set ablaze each time we meet.
My love grows more beautiful with the evil of each passing hour,
my love on the terrace of a cafe
a white hibiscus in her hands,
dressed in the fashion of a new millennium.
My love who will continue when I am gone
with another's laugh, another's eyes,
like flame that leapt between two candles
and endured, lighting up
the blue of the earth.

Orfeo

Orfeo, lo que de él queda (si queda),
lo que aún puede cantar en la tierra,
¿a qué piedra, a cuál animal enternece?
Orfeo en la noche, en esta noche
(su lira, su grabador, su casete),
¿para quién mira, ausculta las estrellas?
Orfeo, lo que de él sueña (si sueña),
la palabra de tanto destino,
¿quién la recibe ahora de rodillas?

Solo, con su perfil en mármol, pasa
por nuestro siglo tronchado y derruido
bajo la estatua rota de una fábula.
Viene a cantar (si canta) a nuestra puerta,
ante todas las puertas. Aquí se queda,
aquí planta su casa y paga su condena
porque nosotros somos el Infierno.

Orpheus

Orpheus, what is left of him (if anything is left)
what still sings on this earth,
in what animal, in what stone does it lie hidden?
Orpheus in the night, in this night
(his lyre, his tape-recorder, his cassette)
for whom does he gaze upward, taking the pulse of the stars?
Orpheus, what dreams in him (if it dreams)
the word of so much destiny,
who kneels now to receive it?

Lonely, his face cast in marble, he moves
across the vanishing ruins of our century
as the broken statue of a myth.
He comes to sing (if there is singing)
at our door, at all the doorways.
Here he is finally staying,
here he has built his house and serves his sentence
since where we are is the land of the dead.

Caballo Real

Aquel caballo que mi padre era
y que después no fue, ¿por dónde se halla?
Aquellas altas crines de batalla
en donde galopé la tierra entera.

Aquel silencio puesto dondequiera
en sus flancos con tactos de muralla;
la silla en que me trajo, donde calla
la filiación fatal de su quimera.

Sé que vine en el trecho de su vida
al espoleado trote de la suerte
con sus alas de noche ya caída,

y aquí me desmontó de un salto fuerte,
hízose sombras y me dio la brida
para que llegue solo hasta la muerte.

The King's Horse

Where can I find the horse my father was
and later was no more?
The long flowing mane ready for battle
on which I galloped the whole earth.

The silence present everywhere
in flanks that felt like walls;
the saddle where he left me, where
the doomed paternity of his dream fell silent.

I know I came into his life
to the cantering rhythm of fate,
its wing-beats of a night already fallen.

He made one last leap and set me down here.
Turning to shadow he handed me the bridle
for me to make it on my own to death.

Partida

Me voy con cada barco de este puerto,
con cada gota azul de oxígeno
entre roncos silbatos.

Me voy a Rotterdam donde ahora cae densa la nieve
y las gaviotas holandesas
hurgando las mercaderías
se posan en los mástiles.

Un camarote me espera en cada barco,
un libro de Li Po para mi travesía;
—búsquenme en Rotterdam, escríbanme
aunque no parta.

Si no salgo a esta hora será en otra;
las naves cambiarán, no mi deseo,
mi deseo está en Rotterdam:
desde aquí con la nieve lo diviso
entre sus casas.

No hay un solo camino sobre el mar
sin su contrario,
no hay manera de estar y no estar donde se viaja.
Si mediara otra senda más simple, más humana,
saldría sin ausentarme,
la nieve me sería cálida al tacto.

En cada barco de este puerto
tengo fletado mi equipaje;
aunque me vean aquí mañana por los muelles,
estoy a bordo:

Departure

I leave with every boat from this port,
with each blue drop of oxygen,
each hoarse whistle.

I'm off to Rotterdam where at this hour
thick snow falls
and dutch seagulls, divebombing the cargo,
stand guard on the masts.

A cabin waits for me on every ship,
a book of Li Po for the crossing –
look for me in Rotterdam, write to me
even if I don't leave.

If I don't leave at this hour it will be some other;
the boats may change, not my longing;
my longing is in Rotterdam:
from here I can make it out
amid the snow between its houses.

There's not one road across the sea
without its opposite,
there's no way of being and not being where you travel.
If there was another path simpler, more human,
I would leave without being absent,
snow would burn in my hands.

In every boat from this port
I've got my bags stashed;
though you see me here tomorrow on the wharves
I'm there on board;

las naves cambiarán, no mi deseo;
—búsquenme en Rotterdam, escríbanme,
mi deseo tiene vuelo de gaviota
y nieve entre sus alas.

the ships may change, not my longing;
– look for me in Rotterdam, write to me;
my longing's the gull in flight,
the snow trapped on its wings.

Álbum de Familia

Ésta que asoma al fondo era tía Adela,
maga del mundo y viva en tantos tiempos
que hasta hoy no sé si existe o si no existe.
De aquel abuelo heredé el nombre. Una carreta
destartalada lo arrancó del pueblo
para enterrarlo lejos. Yo nacería después
y sin embargo lo recuerdo.
Luis, el letrado, se fue pronto
el año de la peste. Dejó cartas, postales,
el mapa de una vaga inocencia.
Verónica es aquella del abanico blanco
y esa altivez que le sentaba bien.
De este José —hubo otros— nadie supo
dónde, cuándo cayera. Erraba solo
gritándole a su sombra en los caminos.
El rey Ricardo se ve mucho más joven
que su muerte. Y acaso así haya sido...
En la perdida tierra de mis ausentes,
este álbum casi invisible que cierro y abro
quema mis párpados velando ante su sueño.
No los despiertes hasta que me reúna
para siempre con ellos en la última página.

Family Album

The one in the background is Aunt Adela,
a worldly witch who lived at so many different times
even today I don't know if she's still here or not.
From this grandfather I inherited my name.
A rickety old oxcart snatched him from his village
to bury him a long way off.
I was born much later and still I remember him.
Luis the lawyer vanished
in the year of the plague. He left behind letters, postcards,
the map of a vague innocence.
Veronica is that one with a white fan
and the disdainful bearing that became her so well.
Of this particular José – there were several others –
no one knows when or where he perished.
He walked around screaming at his shadow on the roadway.
My dear King Richard looks much younger
than his death. And perhaps that's how it was . . .
In the lost land of my absent family
this almost invisible album I open and close
burns my eyelids as they watch over its dream.
Don't wake these portraits
till I can rejoin them forever
on the album's last page.

Dos Rembrandt

Con grumos ocres pudo el viejo Rembrandt
pintar su último rostro. Es un autorretrato
en su final, hecho de encargo
para un joven pintor de 34.
(El mismo Rembrandt visto en otra cara).

Puestos cerca esos cuadros
muestran en igual pose las dos bocas,
unos ojos intensos o vagos,
las manos juntas en el aire
y el tacto de colores
con hondas luces que se rompen
en sordos sollozos apagados...

Rembrandt en la vejez, al dibujarse,
supo ser objetivo. No interfiere
en los estragos de su vida;
ve lo que fue, no añade, no lamenta.
Su alma sólo nos busca por espejo
y sin pedirnos saldo
se acerca en sus dos rostros,
pero ¿quién al mirarlos no se quema?

Two Rembrandts

In lumpy ochres old Rembrandt painted his last face.
It's a self-portrait of his own ending
made on commission
for a young painter of 34.
The same Rembrandt seen in a different face.

Placed side by side these paintings
show two mouths in the same pose,
the eyes intense or vague,
hands that interlace in air,
colours touched by deep flashes
of light that break in stifled dumb sobbing . . .

Rembrandt in his old age, painting himself,
knew how to be objective. He does not interfere
with the ravages of his life;
he sees what was, adds nothing, does not lament.
His soul only seeks us as a mirror
and without asking for our payment
draws close within these two faces,
but looking at them
who doesn't feel his own eyes
getting burned?

Hotel Antiguo

Una mujer a solas se desnuda,
pared por medio, en el hotel antiguo
de esta ciudad remota donde duermo.

Abren las sedas un rumor disperso
que se mezcla al follaje
de los helechos en el aire.

Se oyen llaves que giran en un cofre,
jadeos ahogados, prendas,
la inocencia de gestos solitarios
que beben los espejos.

A su tiempo la noche se desnuda
y las calles apiladas se doblan
en un vasto ropaje
con la fatiga de un final de fiesta.

Una mujer a solas tras los muros,
unos pasos, un oscuro deseo,
hasta mí llega de otro mundo
como alguien que he amado y que me habla
desde algún ataúd lleno de piedras.

Old Hotel

A woman who's there alone takes off her clothes
on the other side of the wall in the old hotel
of this distant city where I am sleeping.

A faint rippling of her undergarments
mingles with the tossing of ferns
stroked by the breeze.

I can hear keys turning in jewellery boxes,
stifled sighs, trinkets falling,
the innocence of solitary gestures
drunk by mirrors.

In its own time the night strips bare.
Streets that wind into streets double over
like an enormous cloak
let fall with all the tiredness of a carnival's ending.

A woman alone on the other side of the wall,
a few steps, an obscure longing,
reaches me from another world
like someone I once loved who now talks to me
from inside a coffin filled with stones.

Setiembre

Mira setiembre: nada se ha perdido
con fiarnos de las hojas.
La juventud vino y se fue. Los árboles no se movieron.
El hermano al morir te quemó en llanto
pero el sol continúa.
La casa fue derrumbada, no su recuerdo.
Mira setiembre con su pala al hombro
cómo arrastra hojas secas.

La vida vale más que la vida, sólo eso cuenta.
Nadie nos preguntó para nacer,
¿qué sabían nuestros padres? ¿Los suyos qué supieron?
Ningún dolor les ahorró sombra y sin embargo
se mezclaron al tiempo terrestre.
Los árboles saben menos que nosotros
y aún no se vuelven.
La tierra va más sola ahora sin dioses
pero nunca blasfema.
Mira setiembre cómo te abre el bosque
y sobrepasa tu deseo.
Abre tus manos, llénalas con estas lentas hojas,
no dejes que una sola se te pierda.

September

Look at September; we have lost nothing
placing our trust in its leaves.
Youth has come and gone, the trees haven't moved.
Your brother's death burnt you with savage flames
but the sun continues.
The house has been torn down, but not its memory.
Look at September with its wicker basket on its shoulder,
how it gathers the dry leaves.

Life is more than life, only that counts.
No one asked us to be born, what did our parents know?
What did their parents know before them?
No pain could stop their transformation into shadows
and yet both were mixed in earthly time.
The trees know less than us
and even they don't return.
The earth is lonelier now without gods
but never blasphemes.
Look at September: how it opens its forests for you
and oversteps your longing.
Open your hands, fill them with these slow leaves,
don't let a single one be lost to you.

Mare Nostrum

El horizonte es intuitivo
pero las palmas a la orilla del mar
se sirven té y hablan de los clásicos.

El horizonte es intuitivo y la noche y los barcos
que a esta hora retornan a puerto
por los confines del Atlántico.

Hay un bar de roída madera
donde el agua se rompe en marejada.
Hay una casa miserable
con el grito de un niño en las paredes,
un grito azul, de náufrago.

La luna ronda blanca e intuitiva
pero las palmas conservan sus gafas.
Abstraídas, prosiguen sus charlas
ante el mar, ante el salobre té del mar,
sorbo tras sorbo y hablan de los clásicos.

Mare Nostrum

The horizon's intuitive
but the palms on the sea's edge
are serving tea and they speak of the classics.

The horizon is intuitive, like the night and the boats
which at this hour return to port
along the Atlantic shoreline.

On a rotten wooden bar
the sea swells and breaks.
There's a run-down house,
a child's cry in its walls,
a blue cry of shipwreck.

The curved white moon is intuitive
but the palm trees still wear sunglasses.
Abstracted, they go on with their chattering
at the sea's edge, before the brackish tea of the ocean,
sip by sip, and they speak of the classics.

Lisboa

a Octavio Paz

También de ti se irá Lisboa,
es decir ya se fue, ya va muy lejos,
con sus colinas de casas blancas,
los celajes de Ulises sobre sus piedras
y la niebla que va y viene entre sus barcos.
Lisboa se fue por esos rumbos del camino
por donde huyó la juventud,
sin que retengas la huella de un guijarro.
Hoy es memoria, ausencia, sueño,
pero palpaste su suelo antes de verla,
su viejo río era esa raya honda
que cruza la palma de tu mano.
Y tal vez si te apresuras la divises,
puede encontrarse tras el muro de ti mismo
donde se expande el horizonte.
Es decir, has de esperarla a cada instante,
suele anunciarse de improviso ante los ojos,
Lisboa se oculta, retorna, va contigo:
hay un jirón de su crepúsculo en la sombra
de quien cruzó una vez sus calles
que lo va acompañando por el mundo
y se aleja con pasos desconocidos.

Lisbon

to Octavio Paz

Lisbon is leaving you too,
that's to say, it's gone, already travels somewhere far off
with the white houses on its hillsides,
Ulysses' sunset skies washed on its stones,
with the fog that comes and goes between its boats.
Lisbon has vanished down the street
where your youth fled
and you don't even retain one pebble's imprint.
Today Lisbon is memory, absence, dream,
but you felt its soil before seeing it.
Its old river's the deep line
crossing the palm of your hand.
And maybe if you hurry you can catch it,
maybe you'll find it on the other side of the wall of yourself
where the horizon steadily grows larger.
You must wait for it at each moment,
it mostly announces itself out of the blue.
Lisbon hides, returns, journeys with you.
There's a shred of its twilight in the shadow
of whoever's just once crossed its streets,
some shred that accompanies him through the world,
then slips away, its footsteps unrecognised.

El Otro

Miro el hombre que soy y que vuelve;
he leído en Heródoto su vida;
me habla arameo, sánscrito, sueco.

Es miope, tardo, subjetivo;
yerra por calles que declinan
hasta que el horizonte lo disuelve.

Conozco sus muertes en el Bósforo,
sus túmulos en Creta,
los sollozos en un portal oscuro
por una mujer muerta en la peste.

Llama a todas las casas de la tierra;
cambia dolor por compañía,
hastío por inocencia,
y de noche se acerca a mi lámpara,
a escribir para que las nubes amanezcan
más al centro del patio,
más cerca del país que nos espera.

The Other

I watch the man I am and the man who returns;
I've read his life in Herodotus;
he speaks Aramaic, Sanskrit, Swedish.

He is myopic, always late, subjective;
he wanders on roads that slope away
until the horizon dissolves him.

I know his deaths in the Bosphorus,
his tombs on Crete,
his sobbing in an unknown doorway
for a woman who died of the plague.

He calls at all the houses of the earth;
changes sorrow for companionship,
indifference for innocence.
By night he approaches my lamp to write
so that the clouds may rise at dawn
nearer to the centre of the patio,
closer to the land that awaits us.

Terredad

Estar aquí por años en la tierra,
con las nubes que lleguen, con los pájaros,
suspensos de horas frágiles.
A bordo, casi a la deriva,
más cerca de Saturno, más lejanos,
mientras el sol da vuelta y nos arrastra
y la sangre recorre su profundo universo
más sagrado que todos los astros.

Estar aquí en la tierra: no más lejos
que un árbol, no más inexplicables;
livianos en otoño, henchidos en verano,
con lo que somos o no somos, con la sombra,
la memoria, el deseo, hasta el fin
(si hay un fin) voz a voz,
casa por casa,
sea quien lleve la tierra, si la llevan,
o quien la espere, si la aguardan,
partiendo juntos cada vez el pan
en dos, en tres, en cuatro,
sin olvidar la parte de la hormiga
que siempre viaja de remotas estrellas
para estar a la hora en nuestra cena,
aunque las migas sean amargas.

Earthdom

To be here a few years on earth
with the clouds that arrive, with the birds
dangling from fragile hours.
On the edge, almost adrift,
closer to Saturn, more distant,
while the sun revolves and drags us with it
and the blood circles once more through the depths of its
      universe
more sacred than the stars.

To be here on earth; no more distant than a tree,
no more inexplicable;
thin in autumn, laden in summer,
with what we are and are not, with shadow,
memory, longing, until the end
(if there is one) voice to voice,
from house to house,
whoever it may be who carries the earth, if they carry it,
or whoever hopes for it, if they keep watch,
each time dividing our common bread
in two, in three, in four,
without forgetting the share for the ant
who is still travelling from remote stars
to be here on time at our table
even though the crumbs are bitter.

Amantes

Se amaban. No estaban solos en la tierra;
tenían la noche, sus vísperas azules,
                    sus celajes.

Vivían uno en el otro, se palpaban
como dos pétalos no abiertos en el fondo
                    de alguna flor del aire.

Se amaban. No estaban solos a la orilla
                    de su primera noche.
                    Y era la tierra la que se amaba en ellos,
                    el oro nocturno de sus vueltas,
                    la galaxia.

Ya no tendrían dos muertes. No iban a separarse.
Desnudos, asombrados, sus cuerpos se tendían
como hileras de luces en un largo aeropuerto
donde algo iba a llegar desde muy lejos,
                    no demasiado tarde.

Lovers

They loved each other. They were not alone on the earth;
they had night, its blue evenings,
                  its sunset clouds.

They lived in the other, they shuddered
like two unopened petals in the depths
                  of some flower of the air.

They loved. They were not alone on the shore
                  of their first night.
                  And it was the earth which loved itself in them,
                  the nightly gold of its rotations,
                  the galaxy.

They would not be two corpses. They were not going to separate.
Naked, startled, their bodies stretched out
like the rows of light in an enormous airport
where something has just arrived from a long way off
                  and not too far behind schedule.

La Tierra Giró para Acercarnos

La tierra giró para acercarnos,
giró sobre sí misma y en nosotros,
hasta juntarnos por fin en este sueño,
como fue escrito en el Simposio.
Pasaron noches, nieves y solsticios;
pasó el tiempo en minutos y milenios.
Una carreta que iba para Nínive
llegó a Nebraska.
Un gallo cantó lejos del mundo,
en la previda a menos mil de nuestros padres.
La tierra giró musicalmente
llevándonos a bordo;
no cesó de girar un solo instante,
como si tanto amor, tanto milagro
sólo fuera un adagio hace mucho ya escrito
entre las partituras del Simposio.

The Earth Turned to Bring Us Closer

The earth turned to bring us closer,
it spun on itself and within us,
and finally joined us together in this dream
as written in the Symposium.
Nights passed by, snowfalls and solstices;
time passed in minutes and millennia.
An ox cart that was on its way to Nineveh
arrived in Nebraska.
A rooster was singing some distance from the world,
in one of the thousand pre-lives of our fathers.
The earth was spinning with its music
carrying us on board;
it didn't stop turning a single moment
as if so much love, so much that's miraculous
was only an adagio written long ago
in the Symposium's score.

La Araña Veloz

Veloz se mueve la araña que nos teje,
desde su estrella remota,
con impalpables filamentos.

Veloz fabrica la piel, la voz, los nervios,
los pasos que nos llevan por el mundo,
el pozo de los sueños, sus enigmas,
y esa música inaudible que nos sigue
mezclando lo corpóreo y lo sonámbulo.

Aquí mismo ya hilvana cifras, letras,
sobre el papel está moviéndome la mano,
desde tan lejos me convierte en su escriba.
Mis libros, esta lámpara, los cuadros,
lo que soy, lo que he sido, el humo del patio,
mi muerte tácita, mis ojos
y los ojos que lleguen a leerme
estamos pendiendo de sus hilos.

The Nimble Spider

Nimbly moves the spider that weaves us
from his distant star
with impalpable filaments.

Speedily he spins the skin, the voice, the nerves,
the steps that carry us through the world,
the well of our dreams, its enigmas,
and that inaudible music which follows us
mixing what belongs to the body
with what belongs to the sleepwalker.

Right here at this minute he is knocking together
figures, letters.
Across this paper he moves my hand,
from so far off turning me into his scribe.
My books, this lamp, the paintings on the wall,
what I am and have been,
the early morning fog curling over the patio,
my implicit death, my eyes
and the eyes that will one day read me,
we all hang suspended from his threads.

En el Café

La tenue lluvia sin dinero
ha llegado de lejos con su armónica
a este Café remoto donde escribo
y aquí y allá puebla los aires
la vaga música de su rumor ausente.

Es la misma de siempre, aunque esta tarde
luzca más joven: se ha cortado el pelo.
Y junto a ella no sé de dónde vuelven
las risas y las voces de hace veinte años,
cuando el Café quedaba en otra calle
y nuestras charlas crecían con el insomnio
hasta volverse ceniza en los espejos...

Pobre como los dioses que vienen a beber
en esta sala donde sólo hay ateos,
y más pobre tal vez, aunque lo oculte,
nos trae de lejos su música un instante,
quizá por gusto, nostalgia o mero hastío,
pero no por dinero.

In the Café

The penniless thin rain
has come from somewhere very far
to the remote Cafe where I am writing –
its cheap harmonica
traces here and there on the breeze
an indescribable music of lost sounds.

The same as always, though tonight
a little younger, its hair clipped short.
And, sitting beside the rain, I don't know where they come
      from,
the voices and laughter of twenty years ago
when the Cafe was in another street
and our conversations, fed by insomnia,
became so much ash in the mirrors.

Poor as the gods who drink
in these bars frequented only by atheists,
even poorer perhaps, though it hides it,
from somewhere very far
the rain brings us its music for a moment,
perhaps because it wants to, or from nostalgia
or pure boredom,
but not for money.

El Rezagado

Por esta calle ya pasó mi entierro
con sus patéticos discursos.
Liviano me llevaban
entre parientes desconocidos.

Una mujer al paso del cortejo
se detuvo a mirarlo
con insinuante azoramiento.
Supe después que era una sombra,
llevaba siglos bajo tierra.

Arriba, monologantes nubes,
acaso un lento avión en vuelo;
abajo, toses, ademanes
y lugares comunes.

Iba dormido e indeciso
en el último viaje.
Era mi despedida de este mundo,
la primera vez que me moría.

Hacia el fin de milenio,
de pronto quedé fuera de grupo,
rezagado, contemplando los árboles.
El entierro, sin mí, prosiguió rumbo
por las penumbras suburbiales.
Lo voy siguiendo ahora desde lejos
al paso de los años.

Left Behind

Down these streets my funeral has just passed
with its pathetic speeches.
Lightly they lifted my body
among unrecognizable relatives.

As the procession passed
a woman stopped and gazed
with flirtatious embarrassment.
Later I realized she was a shadow
already shouldering centuries under earth.

Above the clouds continued their monologues,
a slow plane barely moved in its flight;
below mourners cough, polite gestures of the crowd,
the usual phrases.

Asleep and with no sense of where I was,
I was going on the last journey.
It was my farewell to this world,
the first time that I was going to die.

Towards the end of the millennium
suddenly I found myself outside of the group,
left behind, contemplating the trees.
The funeral, without me, continued on its course
through the shady half-light of suburban streets.
I walk slowly following it now from far off
down the passage of the years

La Poesía

La poesía cruza la tierra sola,
apoya su voz en el dolor del mundo
y nada pide
                              —ni siquiera palabras.

Llega de lejos y sin hora, nunca avisa;
tiene la llave de la puerta.
Al entrar siempre se detiene a mirarnos.
Después abre su mano y nos entrega
una flor o un guijarro, algo secreto,
pero tan intenso que el corazón palpita
demasiado veloz. Y despertamos.

Poetry

Poetry crosses the earth alone,
takes its voice from the suffering of the world
and asks for nothing –
               not even words.

Arriving from a great distance at any hour,
it gives no warning.
It holds the key to the door.
As it enters it stops to gaze about at us.
Later it will open its hand and give us
a flower or a pebble, something secret
but so intense the heart beats
too fast. And we wake.

I like this
image.

my
metaphoric
dreams
are spoken
of here, too

El Buey

El buey que lleva mis huesos por el mundo,
el que arrastra mi sombra,
uncido a las estrellas, a yugos siderales,
va arando el tiempo, no la tierra,
por eso es sabio, profundo, demorado,
al tardo paso de las nubes.
Es mi buey, mi maestro cuadrúpedo,
por quien he conocido en la quietud
el habla porosa de las piedras
y cierta obediencia práctica a las cosas,
casi taoísta.
Es mi buey, la parte móvil de mi estatua,
lento de sol a sol sobre las horas;
el que ara el tiempo, no los campos,
el que graba con surcos en mi rostro
las semanas, los meses y los años.

The Ox

The ox that carries my bones through the world,
who pulls my shadow behind him,
yoked to the stars, strapped in starry harness,
goes back and forth ploughing time, not earth.
For this he is wise, deep, patient,
in tune with the slow passing of clouds.
He is my ox, my four-footed master,
from whom I've learned in quietude
the porous speech of stones
and a certain practical obedience to things,
almost Taoist.
He's my ox, the active half of my statue,
moving slowly from sunrise to sunrise across the hours;
my ox who ploughs time, not the fields,
who carves in the furrows of my face
the weeks, the months, the years.

La Mesa

¿Qué puede una mesa sola
contra la redondez de la tierra?
Ya tiene bastante con que nada se caiga
cuando las sillas entran en voz baja
y en su torno a la hora se congregan.

Si el tiempo amella los cuchillos,
lleva y trae comensales,
varía los temas, las palabras,
¿qué puede el dolor de su madera?

¿Qué puede contra el costo de las cosas,
contra el ateísmo de la cena,
de la Última Cena?

Si el vino se derrama, si el pan falta
y los hombres se tornan ausentes,
¿qué puede sino estar inmóvil, fija,
entre el hambre y las horas,
con qué va a intervenir aunque desee?

Table

compassion for the inanimate

What can a single table do
against the roundness of the earth?
It has its work cut out to make sure nothing falls
when the chairs come inside mumbling
and draw together for supper.

As time dents the knives,
brings in and carries out new faces round the table,
changes the décor, the words,
what use is the suffering of wood?

What can a table do against the drift of things,
against the atheism of all suppers,
of the last supper?

If the wine spills, if the bread is missing
and the guests turn into ghosts,
what can a table do but sit there
stranded in stillness
between hunger and time?
What can it do to change a thing
however great its desire?

Mural Escrito por el Viento

a Jesús Sanoja Hernández

Adora a tu ciudad pero no mucho tiempo,
olvida el tacto de sus piedras,
sé gentil a tu paso y prosigue de largo,
no proyectes quedarte entre sus muros
hasta fundirte en el paisaje.
Una ciudad no es fiel a un río ni a un árbol,
mucho menos a un hombre.

Quien amó una ciudad solamente en la tierra,
casa por casa, bajo soles o lluvias
y fue por años tatuándola en sus ojos,
sabe cómo engañan de pronto sus colinas,
cómo se tornan crueles esas tardes doradas
que tanto nos seducen.

Las ciudades se prometen al que llega,
pero no aman a nadie.
Cuando se ven por la ventana de un avión
todas atraen
con sus cumbres azules
y largos bulevares rumorosos,
pero al tiempo son sombras amargas.
Sus edificios nos vuelven solitarios,
sus cementerios están llenos de suicidas
que no dejaron ni una carta.
Por eso el río pasa y no vuelve,
por eso el árbol que crece a sus orillas
elige siempre la madera más leve
y termina de barco.

Mural Written by the Wind

to Jesús Sanoja Hernández

Adore your city but not for too long;
forget the touch of its stones;
tread lightly as you go and continue your journey.
Don't long to stay at home between its walls
till you plant yourself in its landscape.
A city isn't faithful to a river or a tree
much less a man.

Anyone who's loved one city alone on earth,
house by house, under sun or rain,
and spent years tattooing it on his eyes,
knows how without warning its hills betray us,
how cruel can be those shining afternoons
that seduced us so much.

Cities promise themselves to every new arrival
but love no one.
When seen through the windows of a plane
all of them draw you in
with their blue heights
and long noisy boulevards,
but with time they become bitter shadows.
Their buildings make us lonely.
Their cemeteries are full of suicides
who didn't even leave behind a note.
That's why the river flows by and doesn't return.
That's why the tree that grows on its bank
chooses the lightest wood
and ends up a boat.

Un Canto para el Tordo

Un canto para el tordo que viene a amanecer
soñando aún, junto a nosotros,
y más que nadie contento de estar vivo.

Al mañanero amigo, negro en lo blanco,
con amplias plumas de paraguas
y patas como elipsis de un escriba.
El solitario, el músico,
que me esquiva azorándose en la calle
si me acerco
y se repliega cubriendo entre las alas
el piano de sí mismo.

Antes que arome mi primer café
en la taza del día
y el árbol lo reclame de lejos a su nido,
un canto para el tordo, el inocente,
no importa que apenas me comprenda,
que sólo alcance a descifrar mi voz mañana,
en otro amanecer, en otra vida.

A Song for the Blackbird

A song for the blackbird who arrives at dawn,
still dreamy just like us
and, more than any of us, happy to be alive.

Friend to the early riser, black in all the whiteness,
his wings stretch wide as an umbrella,
his feet the staccato shorthand of a scribe.
Solitary one, musician,
flustered, he dodges me in the street if I come close
and shies away, hiding under his wings
the piano of himself.

Before the scent of my first coffee
in its cup of daylight,
before the tree recalls him to his far-off nest,
a song for the blackbird, the bird of innocence,
and it doesn't matter that he hardly understands me,
that he could only decode my morning voice
in another dawn,
a different life.

Despertar

La luz derrumba los castillos
donde flotábamos en sueño;
queda su tufarada de ballena
en nuestro espejo opaco...
Ya erramos cerca de Saturno,
ahora la tierra gira más despacio.
Temblamos solos en el medio del mundo
y abrimos la ventana
para que el día pase en su barco.
Anoche nos dormimos en un país tan lejano.

Waking Up

Light drowns us as we lie floating in sleep;
its beached-whale stench clouds our dull mirror.
We'd just been wandering close to Saturn,
now the earth turns more slowly in its curve.
Alone at the centre of the world
we shiver and open the window
so the day in its boat may drift on by.
By night we sleep in such a distant country.

La Casa

En la mujer, en lo profundo de su cuerpo
      se construye la casa,
       entre murmullos y silencios.
Hay que acarrear sombras de piedras,
     leves andamios,
     imitar a las aves.

Especialmente cuando duerme
     y en el sueño sonríe
       —nivelar hacia el fondo,
     no despertarla;
seguir el declive de sus formas,
los movimientos de sus manos.

Sobre las dunas que cubren su sueño
      en convulso paisaje,
       hay que elevar altas paredes,
fundar contra la lluvia, contra el viento,
     años y años.

Un ademán a veces fija un muro,
de algún susurro nace una ventana,
desmontamos errantes a la puerta
      y atamos el caballo.

Al fondo de su cuerpo la casa nos espera
y la mesa servida con las palabras limpias
para vivir, tal vez para morir,
     ya no sabemos,
porque al entrar nunca se sale.

The House

In woman, in the depths of her body,
between whispered words and silences
a house is built.
You must lift and carry
       the darkness of stone,
       the lightness of scaffolding.
You must imitate the birds.

Especially when she sleeps
       and in her dreams smiles,
       smooth out all the deep hollows.
       Do not awake her
but follow the curves of her form,
the movement of her hands.

Along the dunes which cover her sleep
       in a trembling landscape,
       erect the high sweep of floorboards.
Build against rain, against wind,
       build for years and years.

Sometimes a gesture will secure a wall.
From a sigh a window is born.
After long journeys we dismount at the doorway
       to tie up a tired horse.

In the depths of her body the house awaits us
and the table laid out with its pure words
for living or for dying
       we no longer know which
since no one who enters this house
ever leaves.

Tiempo Transfigurado

a António Ramos Rosa

La casa donde mi padre va a nacer
no está concluida,
le falta una pared que no han hecho mis manos.

Sus pasos que ahora me buscan por la tierra
vienen hacia esta calle.
No logro oírlos, todavía no me alcanzan.

Detrás de aquella puerta se oyen ecos
y voces que a leguas reconozco,
pero son dichas por los retratos.

El rostro que no se ve en ningún espejo
porque tarda en nacer o ya no existe,
puede ser de cualquiera de nosotros
—a todos se parece.

En esa tumba no están mis huesos
sino los del bisnieto Zacarías,
que usaba bastón y seudónimo.
Mis restos ya se perdieron.

Este poema fue escrito en otro siglo,
por mí, por otro, no recuerdo,
alguna noche junto a un cabo de vela.
El tiempo dio cuenta de la llama
y entre mis manos quedó a oscuras
sin haberlo leído.
Cuando vuelva a alumbrar ya estaré ausente.

Transfigured Time

to António Ramos Rosa

The house where my father will be born
is still unfinished.
It lacks the wall my hands have not yet built.

His footsteps searching for me across the earth
now come towards this street.
Yet I can't hear them, they still don't reach me.

Behind that door are echoes
and voices I recognise miles off,
but they are spoken only by portraits.

The face not seen in any mirror,
because it's late being born
or still doesn't exist,
could be of any one of us –
it looks like all of us.

My bones are not in that tomb
but those of Zacarias, the great-grandson,
who used a walking stick and pseudonym.
My own remains have long been lost.

This poem was written in another century,
some night by a guttering candle,
by me, by someone else, I don't recall.
Time consumed the flame
and lingered in my darkened hands
and in these eyes that never read the poem.
When the candle returns with its light
I'll already be gone.

Manoa

No vi a Manoa, no hallé sus torres en el aire,
ningún indicio de sus piedras.

Seguí el cortejo de sombras ilusorias
que dibujan sus mapas.
Crucé el río de los tigres
y el hervor del silencio en los pantanos.
Nada vi parecido a Manoa
ni a su leyenda.

Anduve absorto detrás del arco iris
que se curva hacia el sur y no se alcanza.
Manoa no estaba allí, quedaba a leguas de esos mundos
—siempre más lejos.

Ya fatigado de buscarla me detengo,
¿qué me importa el hallazgo de sus torres?
Manoa no fue cantada como Troya
ni cayó en sitio
ni grabó sus paredes con hexámetros.
Manoa no es un lugar
sino un sentimiento.
A veces en un rostro, un paisaje, una calle
su sol de pronto resplandece.
Toda mujer que amamos se vuelve Manoa
sin darnos cuenta.
Manoa es la otra luz del horizonte,
quien sueña puede divisarla, va en camino,
pero quien ama ya llegó, ya vive en ella.

Manoa

I did not see Manoa,
never found its towers in the air
or any sign of its stones.

I followed the cortege of illusory shadows
that draw its maps.
I crossed the river of tigers
and the boiling silence of the swamps.
I saw nothing similar to Manoa
or its legend.

I travelled absorbed behind the rainbow
that curves towards the south and never ends.
Manoa was not there, it was still miles and miles from those
        worlds –
always further off.

Exhausted now from searching I rest.
What would the discovery of its towers mean after all?
Manoa was never sung like Troy.
Its buildings never collapsed in one particular site.
Its walls were never engraved in hexameters.
Manoa is not a place
but a sentiment.
At times its sun unexpectedly shines
in a face, a landscape, a street.
Every woman we love becomes Manoa
whether we realize this or not.
Manoa's the horizon's other light.
Whoever dreams can make it out, heads off towards it,
but whoever loves is there already
and lives within her.

Canción

Cada cuerpo con su deseo
y el mar al frente.
Cada lecho con su naufragio
y los barcos al horizonte.

Estoy cantando la vieja canción
que no tiene palabras.
Cada cuerpo junto a otro cuerpo,
cada espejo temblando en la sombra
y las nubes errantes.

Estoy tocando la antigua guitarra
con que los amantes se duermen.
Cada ventana en sus helechos,
cada cuerpo desnudo en su noche
y el mar al fondo, inalcanzable.

Song

Each body with its longings
and the sea opposite.
Each bed with its shipwreck
and the boats on the horizon.

I am singing the old song
that has no words.
Each body lying next to another body,
each mirror trembling in darkness
and the clouds adrift.

I play on the old guitar
the tune lovers fall asleep to.
Each window with its trellis of green vines,
each body naked in its night
and the sea in its depths, unreachable.

La Vida

a Vicente Gerbasi

La Vida toma aviones y se aleja;
sale de día, de noche, a cada instante
hacia remotos aeropuertos.

La Vida se va, se fue, llega más tarde;
es difícil seguirla: tiene horarios
imprevistos, secretos;
cambia de ruta, sueña a bordo, vuela.

La Vida puede llegar ahora, no sabemos,
puede estar en Nebraska, en Estambul,
o ser esa mujer que duerme
en la sala de espera.

La Vida es el misterio en los tableros,
los viajantes que parten o regresan,
el miedo, la aventura, los sollozos,
las nieblas que nos quedan del adiós
y los aviones puros que se elevan
hacia los aires altos del deseo.

Life

to Vicente Gerbasi

Life boards planes and heads off into the distance;
by day, by night, at every instant
it's leaving for some remote airport.

Life goes away, disappears, comes back later on.
It's hard to follow life:
it keeps secretive unpredictable hours,
changes itinerary, sleeps right through the trip,
goes on flying.

Life could be arriving now, we don't know,
it might be in Nebraska or Istambul
or maybe it's that woman asleep opposite us
in the transit lounge.

Life's the unknown on the board of destinations,
the travellers who leave or return,
fear, adventure, weeping,
the clouds that wait for us beyond the good-byes
and the pure planes that lift
towards the high winds of desire.

Vecindad

Mi cuerpo errante se fatiga
de llevarme despacio por la tierra,
de andar conmigo horas y horas,
caviloso, al lado de su huésped.

A veces dócil se detiene
para suplirme un ademán, un gesto;
después se suelta de mis manos,
se distrae contemplando las piedras...

Así paseamos juntos la ciudad,
absortos, hostiles en secreto,
él con la forma de mis padres,
su sangre, su materia,
yo con lo que queda de su sueño;
los dos tan cerca que los pasos
se nos confunden en la niebla.

Closeness

My body's a tired hobo,
weary of bearing me slowly over this earth,
of wandering moody hour by hour
at its guest's side.

Sometimes it quietly stops
to give me a nod or a gesture;
later it slips out of my hands,
wanders off, starts staring at stones ...

In this way together we stroll through the city,
self-absorbed, hiding our hatred;
he with my parents' shape,
their blood, their substance,
I with what's left of their dream;
the two of us so close
in the mist we can't tell our steps apart.

Algunas Palabras

Algunas de nuestras palabras
son fuertes, francas, amarillas,
otras redondas, lisas, de madera...
Detrás de todas queda el Atlántico.

Algunas de nuestras palabras
son barcos cargados de especias;
vienen o van según el viento
y el eco de las paredes.

Otras tienen sombras de plátanos,
vuelos de raudos azulejos.
El año madura en los campos
sus resinas espesas.

Palmeras de lentos jadeos
giran al fondo de lo que hablamos,
sollozos en casas de barro
de nuestras pobres conversas.

Algunas de nuestras palabras
las inventan los ríos, las nubes.
De su tedio se sirve la lluvia
al caer en las tejas.

Así pasa la vida y conversamos
dejando que la lengua vaya y vuelva.
Unas son fuertes, francas, amarillas,
otras redondas, lisas, de madera...
Detrás de todas queda el Atlántico.

A Few Words

A few of our words
are strong, forthright, yellow,
others full-bodied, smooth, made of wood . . .
Behind them all lies the Atlantic.

A few of our words
are boats laden with spice;
they come and go with the wind
like echoes between walls.

Others are shady banana palms,
impatient birds in flight.
In the fields the year ripens
its heavy resins.

Palm trees with their slow sighs
stir in the depths of our speech,
the sobbing in mud-brick houses
of all our thin talk.

Some of our words
are invented by rivers and clouds;
falling on roof tiles
the rain borrows their tedium.

And so life passes and we converse
letting language come and go.
Some words are strong, forthright, yellow,
others full-bodied, smooth, made of wood . . .
Behind them all lies the Atlantic.

Adiós al Siglo XX

a Álvaro Mutis

Cruzo la calle Marx, la calle Freud;
ando por una orilla de este siglo,
despacio, insomne, caviloso,
espía *ad honorem* de algún reino gótico,
recogiendo vocales caídas, pequeños guijarros
tatuados de rumor infinito.
La línea de Mondrian frente a mis ojos
va cortando la noche en sombras rectas
ahora que ya no cabe más soledad
en las paredes de vidrio.
Cruzo la calle Mao, la calle Stalin;
miro el instante donde muere un milenio
y otro despunta su terrestre dominio.
Mi siglo vertical y lleno de teorías...
Mi siglo con sus guerras, sus posguerras
y su tambor de Hitler allá lejos,
entre sangre y abismo.
Prosigo entre las piedras de los viejos suburbios
por un trago, por un poco de jazz,
contemplando los dioses que duermen disueltos
en el serrín de los bares,
mientras descifro sus nombres al paso
y sigo mi camino.

Farewell to the Twentieth Century

to Alvaro Mutis

I cross Marx street, Freud plaza,
I walk along one shore of this century,
moody, slow, insomniac,
honorary spy for some gothic realm,
gathering up the big fallen letters, small pebbles
chipped and rounded by infinite echoes.
Opposite me the Mondrian line
cuts night into dark squares
now there's no more solitude
behind glass walls.
I cross Mao street, Stalin street;
I watch the instant where one millennium dies
and another launches its earthly dominion.
My upright century full of theories . . .
My century of wars and postwars
and Hitler's drum over there in the distance
between blood and abyss.
I move on along the old suburbs' cobblestones
for a shot of scotch, a little jazz,
watching the washed-up gods asleep
in sawdust bars,
as en-passant I decipher their names
and continue my journey.

Elegía a la Muerte de mi Hermano Ricardo

Mi hermano ha muerto, sus huesos yacen
caídos en el polvo. Sin ojos con qué llorar,
me habla triste, se sienta en su muerte
y me abraza con su llanto sepultado.

Mi hermano, el rey Ricardo, murió una mañana
en un hospital de ciudad, víctima
de su corazón que trajo a la vida
fatales dolencias de familia.

Mi madre estuvo una semana muerta junto a él
y regresó con sus ojos apaleados
para mirarme de frente. Aún hay tierra
y llanto de Ricardo en sus ojos.

Perdía voz —dijo mi hermana, tenía febricitancia
de elegido y nos miraba con tanta compasión
que lloramos hasta su última madrugada.
Mamá es más pobre ahora, mucho más pobre.

Mi familia lo cercó. El nos amaba
con la nariz taponada de algodones.
Todos éramos piedras y mirábamos
un río que comenzaba a pasar.

Lo llevaron alzado como un ave de augurios
y lo sembraron en la tierra amorosa
donde la muerte cuida a los jóvenes.
Cuando bajó, sollozaba profundo.

Elegy for the Death of my Brother Ricardo

My brother is dead, his bones
are fallen in the dust. Without eyes to weep,
he speaks to me sadly, regrets his death,
embraces me with buried weeping.

My brother, king Richard, died one morning
in a city hospital, victim of
a heart that brought into his life
fatal family sufferings.

My mother lay dead for a whole week beside him
and came back, her eyes beaten,
to look straight at me.
Even now there's earth
and Ricardo's tears in her eyes.

"He's lost his voice", my sister said. He had the raging fever
of someone marked, gazing at us with such compassion
we wept till his last dawn.
Mother is poorer now, much poorer.

My family surrounded him. He loved us,
his nose swathed in cottonwool.
We were all struck dumb like stones
and gazed at a river that began flowing by.

They took him like a bird of prophecy
and sowed him in loving earth
where death shelters the young.
His sobbing streamed from the deep hole he was entering.

El rey Ricardo está muerto. Sus pasos
de oro amargo resuenan en mi sangre
donde caminan con fragor de tormenta.
Su nombre estalla en mi boca como la luz.

Todos lo amamos, mi madre más que todos,
y en su vientre nos reunimos en un llanto compacto:
desde allí conversamos, como las piedras,
con un río que comienza a pasar.

King Richard is dead. A bitter gold, his steps
echo in my blood where they pace
and roar.
His name floods my mouth like light.

We all loved him, my mother more than any of us.
In her womb we're bound together in one single tight weeping;
from that place we talk, like stones,
with a river that's begun to pass by.

El Inocente

Dios me movió los días uno tras otro,
dio vueltas con sus soles hasta paralizarme
como un gallo ante un círculo de tiza.
Me quedé inmóvil viendo girar el mundo
en esferas errantes y volátiles
aquí en mi cuerpo y afuera entre las cosas.
Cambió de casas la ciudad, de calles,
y entre las calles el rumor de las voces
como si cada ser no fuera sino ausencia.
Mudó mi rostro, el tiempo de mi rostro,
pero continué impávido en el centro
con el desamparo de una estatua
que ignora las grietas de sus piedras.
Jamás di un paso,
nunca empujé mi vida hacia la muerte.
Fue Dios el que movió todos mis días,
la redondez de Dios que no da tregua.

The Simple Minded One

to José Bento

God moved my days one by one,
made his suns turn and turn till I was paralysed
like a rooster before a chalk circle.
I stood there motionless seeing the world spin
in wandering erratic spheres
here within my body and out there among things.
He changed the city's houses, its streets,
the murmur of voices in those streets
as if each being was only ever absence.
He altered my face, the age of my face
but I kept on fearless at the centre
helpless as a statue
unaware of the cracks in its stones.
I never took one step,
never gave my life one push towards death.
It was God who moved all my days,
the whole wide roundness of God
that never lets up.

Nana para Emilio

Duerme, hijo mío, que la tierra está sola
y se fueron volando los astros.
Ya el sol guardó su última vela,
se durmieron las llamas;
se durmieron las horas del reloj, no hay tiempo,
no está despierto nadie.
Los hombres dejaron sus cuerpos y partieron;
desde esta calle no se ven,
ya van muy adelante.
El gallo que oyes cantar está muy lejos,
el sueño es su único plumaje.
Duerme, hijo mío, en mi carne, en mis ojos,
como dormiste antes que yo naciera,
como dormimos durante tanto tiempo
dentro de nuestros padres.
Mañana vuelve el día
junto a las voces que nos borró la ausencia
y saldrán del espejo rostros, casas, colinas
y el humo tan humano del café
que viene a despertarnos con hondas vaharadas
—aquí o en otra parte.

Lullaby for Emilio

Sleep, my son, the earth's alone,
and the stars have flown and left us.
Now the sun's put away its last candle,
the flames have gone to sleep;
the clock's hours have gone to sleep, there's no time,
no one's awake.
Men have left their bodies and wandered off;
you can't see them from this street,
they've gone too far ahead.
The rooster you hear singing is very far away,
sleepiness is its only plumage.
Sleep, my son, in my flesh, in my eyes,
as you slept before I was born,
as we slept for so long
within our parents.
Tomorrow day returns
and the voices absence had wiped out –
hills, houses, faces
will tumble from the mirror
and the so-human scent of coffee
that comes to wake us with its deep mists
– here or in some other place.

Al Fin de Todo

Y al fin de todo, si algún fin existe,
no quedarán palabras, son inventos
del hombre iluso que inventó la tierra;
ni tierra alguna, que fue invento del cosmos
tras expandirse los cúmulos del magma;
ni el vasto cosmos que inventó la nada
al trasmutarse en efímera materia;
ni la nada tampoco que fue invento de Dios,
ni el mismo Dios que es invento del tiempo...

No quedará nada de nadie ni de nada
sino el tiempo tras sí mismo dando vueltas;
el tiempo solo, invento de un invento,
que fue inventado también por otro invento,
que fue inventado también por otro invento,
que fue...

At the End of Everything

At the end of everything, if an end exists,
there won't be words, the inventions
of deluded man, himself invented by the earth;
nor anything of earth that was invented by the cosmos
as it expanded in cumulus clouds of magma;
nor the vast cosmos that was invented by nothingness
as it changed itself into ephemeral matter;
nor nothingness either that was invented by God
nor God himself who is time's invention.

Nothing will remain of anyone or anything
but time circling and circling through itself;
time alone, invention of an invention,
that was invented also by another invention,
that was invented also by another invention,
that was . . .

Noches de Trasatlántico

Noches de trasatlántico,
para quien va, para quien vuelve
a bordo, oyendo crujir el maderamen.
Noches del que busca a sus padres
en el agua
y acodado en el puente descubre
que está en el mundo solo
como un astro.
Tufaradas de claraboya,
vaivén insomne de las horas en viaje.
Afuera sólo existe horizonte
cuando sacude sus alas el relámpago.
Sin tregua
arde la lámpara de Supervielle
hasta el fin de la madrugada.
En el pasaporte de su doble
(o su fantasma)
la palabra Montevideo
es el tatuaje de una quimera
que aparece en todas las páginas.

Nights on the Transatlantic

Nights on the Transatlantic
for those setting out,
for those returning,
on board, hearing the timber creak . . .
Nights of a man who seeks his forefathers in water
and, leaning over the rails, discovers
he's alone in the world
like a star.
Sickly smells from the porthole,
sleepless rocking of the hours in their journey.
Outside nothing but the horizon
when the lightning beats its wings.
Without a pause
Supervielle's light burns till dawn.
In his double's passport
(or his ghost's)
the word Montevideo
is the tattoo of a dream
that's there on every page.

Palabras de Boyero

Escribo muy lento, muy lento,
muevo una palabra y después la otra.
Mi lápiz a paso de quelonio,
mi corazón con sus latidos póstumos.
La tierra gravita y no me espera.
Algunos pájaros se quedan en el aire
demorados detrás de sus cuerpos;
nunca puedo alcanzarlos,
pero viajo con ellos.
El dios en que creo todavía no ha nacido,
a su tiempo sabrá revelarse,
no necesita mi creencia.
Escribo muy lento, muy lento,
la ciudad donde viven mis lectores
queda en otro milenio;
voy a su encuentro en mi carro boyero,
si apuro la marcha me atasco en la nieve.

The Ox Driver's Words

I write very slowly, very slowly,
I move one word and then the next.
My pencil at snail's pace,
my heart with its posthumous beats.
The earth spins and doesn't wait for me.
A few birds stay in the air
held back after their bodies;
I can never catch them
yet I travel with them.
The god in whom I believe hasn't yet been born.
In his own time he'll know how to reveal himself,
he doesn't need my belief.
I write very slowly, very slowly.
The city where my readers live
is in another millennium;
I go to meet it in my oxcart.
If I hurry the speed I get stuck in the snow.

La Hora de Hamlet

Esta mañana me sorprende
con mi olvidada calavera entre las manos.
Hago de Hamlet.

Es la hora reductiva del monólogo
en que interrogo a mi Hacedor
sobre esta máscara que ha de volverse polvo,
sobre este polvo que sigue hablando todavía
aquí y acaso en otra parte.

A la distancia que me encuentre de la muerte,
hago de Hamlet.

Hamlet y pájaro con vértigo de alturas,
tras las almenas del íngrimo castillo
que cada quien erige piedra a piedra
para ser o no ser según la suerte,
el destino, la sombra, los pasos del fantasma.

Hamlet's Hour

Morning surprises me,
my forgotten skull in my hands.
I'm playing Hamlet.

It's the all-simplifying hour of the monologue
where I question my Maker
about this mask that will return to dust,
about the dust that will go on talking
here and maybe somewhere else.

At whatever distance I stand from my own death
I'm playing Hamlet.

Hamlet and a bird afraid of heights
above the battlements of that isolate castle
each of us builds stone by stone
to be or not to be left up to chance,
to destiny or darkness, the ghost's footsteps.

Un Tordo

a Leopoldo Iríbarren

Sobre el pretil del patio un tordo,
un tordo negro.
Pájaro urbano, serio, a quien preocupa,
más que las migas de este noviembre,
más que el bullicio de tantos tertuliantes,
la última traducción de Heráclito
a su alfabeto alado. —Y en ello piensa,
en ello
ahora
está pensando...
Devoto de su cátedra,
con su sonoro griego monosilábico,
llenas de tiza sus plumas de maestro,
tan taciturno en esta hora de la tierra,
medita absorto desde su muro.
Pájaro que no lleva pajuelas a su nido
ni ramillas salvajes,
sino finos hexámetros,
algún papiro aún indescifrable
y las visiones del sueño presocrático.

A Thrush

to Leopoldo Iribarren

On the patio railing a thrush,
a black thrush.
Sombre-faced city bird,
more than the crumbs of this November,
more than the racket of a
chattering intelligentsia,
absorbed by its latest translation of Heraclitus
into a winged alphabet – the alphabet of its thoughts
in which
this very moment
it is thinking . . .
Faithful to its seat,
with its sonorous monosyllabic Greek,
its professorial feathers lined with chalk dust,
so sparse its speech
in this hour of the world.
Absorbed it meditates
on its wall.
Bird that doesn't bring to its nest
straw or rough twigs,
but these delicate hexameters –
some still indecipherable papyrus,
what was glimpsed once
in presocratic sleep.

Adiós a mi Padre

Mi padre muerto iba delante
y detrás junio, de verdor ubérrimo,
y la geórgica lluvia venida desde lejos.
Al paso de su sombra
los refrenados carruajes nos seguían.
Mi padre hablaba del camino,
de cafetales con piel de adormidera
que a un simple roce ya eran calles y torres.
Hablaba dormido,
con voz inubicable,
una voz rápida de cuando era muy joven
y yo no había nacido...
Atravesamos un bosque de apamates
que en lenta fila también iban marchando
no sé adónde.
Después sólo se oyeron las cigarras
estremecidas en un coro compacto.
Mi padre acaso creyó que las oía
pero ya entonces a bordo de un relámpago
su alma cruzaba remotas intemperies.

Saying Goodbye to my Father

My dead father was waiting for the June
that is behind him, its green beyond green,
and the earth-warm rain that comes from so far.
As his shadow passed
reined-in horse-carts followed us.
My father spoke of his journey,
of coffee-plantations fragrant as the skin of poppies
that a mere touch would turn to streets and towers.
He was talking in his sleep,
his voice scattered all around me,
racing ahead of itself
like when he was very young
and I was not yet born . . .
We passed a row of apemate trees
which also were walking in slow file
I don't know where.
Later all that could be heard were the cicadas,
their songs merged into a single choir.
My father could scarcely believe he was listening to them
but just then, at the lightning's edge,
his soul was moving through
distant stormclouds.

Final de Lluvia

Ya ennegrecen los árboles
sus ramas y sus flores
al fin del aguacero.

En la terraza del Café
una sombra amontona las sillas
donde rondan amores bisiestos.

Las últimas gotas en las hojas
lavan las plumas del tordo
que ya por hoy no quiere vuelo.

Pasan parejas con paraguas.
Pasan paraguas sin parejas.

End of the Rain

Now the trees darken
their branches and flowers
as the downpour ends.

On the café terrace
a shadow piles up the chairs
where the laziest of lovers hang out.

In the leaves the last drops
wash the feathers of a blackbird
who's done with flying for today.

Couples with umbrellas pass by.
Umbrellas without couples pass by.

Medianoche

Escribo tarde, es medianoche.
Ignoro cuándo he remontado este camino,
cómo llegué donde me encuentro, qué buscaba.
La Cruz del Sur ya se ha corrido al centro
de la radiante soledad nocturna.
No estoy seguro aquí de nada, ni de estos gallos
que alrededor se desgañitan.
Escribo tarde. Los gallos cantan demasiado,
cantan por Esculapio, por Sócrates, por Cristo
y por el viejo Eduardo,
a quien siempre despiertan en su tumba
para que distribuya ahora sus gritos
como si fueran las migas de un relámpago.

Midnight

I write late. It's midnight.
I don't know when I climbed back up this road,
how I got to where I am, what I was seeking.
The Southern Cross has reached the centre
of the night's luminous loneliness.
Here I am sure of nothing, not even the roosters
that set off their noisy din all around.
I write late. The roosters sing too much,
they sing for Esculapius, for Socrates, for Christ,
and for Eduardo, my old man,
whom they keep waking in his grave
so that now he scatters their cries
like crumbs of lightning.

Los Ausentes

Viajan conmigo mis amigos muertos.
Adonde llego, van por todas partes,
apresurados me siguen, me preceden,
gentiles, cómodos e incómodos,
en grupo, solos, conversando, paseando.
A mi paso se mezclan sus huidizos colores
hasta envolverme en un lento crepúsculo...
Tantos y tantos, cada quien en su estatua,
y en torno siempre las máscaras del sueño.
Y mi estatua también a su lado, flotando.
Muertos de nunca habernos muerto,
de estar en algún tiempo, en algún parque,
juntos y apartes, conformes, inconformes,
mudos, charlando, con voces, sin voces,
en verdad ya ni vivos ni muertos:
algo intermedio que tampoco es estatua,
aunque tengamos ya de piedra los ojos
y unos y otros nos sigamos, corteses, polémicos,
contentos de estar en la tierra y de no estar en ella,
en eternas tertulias donde, se hable o no se hable,
todo queda para después o para antes,
para cuando no sabíamos que después era entonces
ni que nuestras sombras de pronto levitaban
visibles e invisibles en el aire.

∼

The Absent Ones

My friends who are dead are travelling with me.
Each place I go they're there, they're all around,
dashing wildly to catch up, they're way ahead,
in comfort, in discomfort, in great style,
in groups, alone, talking, out walking.
Their fleeting colours so blended with my steps
they wrap me in a slow twilight.
More and more of them, each fixed in his statue
and round them at all times the masks of sleep.
And my statue there beside them, floating past.
Dead from never having died,
from being a certain moment, in some park,
together, separated, behaving, misbehaving,
tongue-tied and babbling on, out-loud, in whispers,
neither really living nor dead:
some halfway thing that's not a statue either
though our eyes turn to stone
and each of us follows the other,
diplomatic, polemic,
happy to be on earth and not to be there,
in endless discussions where, speaking or silent,
all's left for later or earlier,
for the hour when no one knew that later
was already then,
when none of us saw how our shadows were suddenly rising,
visible and invisible,
into the air.

~

Un instante de nuevo me reúno con ellos,
conversando otra vez esta tarde, tan tarde,
en un Café de ruidos urbanos, suburbanos...
Es decir, bebiendo sin beber, un poco abstemios,
pues los muertos no beben, pero beben a veces,
juntos y alegres, aunque no tanto, sino alegres,
con un trago o ninguno, pero con un trago,
creyendo que el tiempo ya pasó y no ha pasado,
y por eso pasó sin pasar, es decir, nunca pasa.
Cada quien con un whisky sin hielo o con hielo,
más cálido que frío, sin instante un instante,
con el recuerdo que nada recuerda esta tarde
y por eso se acuerda ahora de todo...
Bebiendo con ellos que fuman y charlan,
que parten y vuelven, dialogan, discuten,
hablando por hablar y a veces por no hablar,
hasta decirnos qué de Picasso hay en la ausencia,
cuánto cubismo en la manera de alejarnos,
el modo de mirarnos con ojos verticales
y saludarnos con la mano a la inversa,
la forma de beber un solo vaso roto
que ya no tiene vidrio ni licor ni volumen,
el modo de no beber creyendo que se bebe
y seguir todos juntos ahora que estoy solo.

For a moment once more I reunite with them,
chatting one more time so late this night,
in a café with its urban, its suburban sounds . . .
Drinking without drinking, rather abstemious,
for the dead don't drink, or else they sometimes drink,
together and happy, not completely so, but happy,
with a stiff drink or stone-sober, better with a drink,
believing time's gone by and hasn't passed –
and so passed us without passing, that is never passes.
And each of us holds a whisky, straight or with ice,
warm more than cold, timeless for a time,
remembering how nothing of this afternoon is remembered
and so he remembers everything.
Drinking with those who chat and smoke,
who leave and return, who dialogue and discuss,
speaking for the sake of speaking or to avoid all speech,
so, in the end, we start saying how much Picasso there is in
        absence,
how much cubism in our way of separating –
this method of seeing ourselves through vertical eyes,
greeting each other, our hands spun round in space,
the correct way to drink from a broken cup
that, by now, has no glass, no liquor and no shape,
how not to drink and believe you're still drinking,
and (always) how to stay together with everyone
now I am alone.

Al Retorno

No sé si entonces era otoño,
el apócrifo otoño de estos trópicos,
no guardo rastro de esos días.
De cualquier estación, sea la que fuere,
no queda por caer hoja ninguna.
La vida jugó sus propias cartas:
—nada salió, tal vez, como yo quise
ni dejó de salir como no quise,
porque no quise nada.
Tras tantos años vuelvo a reencontrarme
con lo que queda, si algo queda,
de la ciudad que amaron mis mayores
al pie de la montaña.
En la hojarasca se oyen murmullos de oro
que amontona la tarde.
Pronto hará frío.
El Ávila me salve.

Coming Back

I don't know if it was autumn then,
the apocryphal autumn of the tropics.
I keep no trace of those days.
Of whatever season it might have been
not a single leaf remains to fall.
Life played its usual cards –
nothing turned out the way I wanted,
and nothing failed to be as I wanted
for I wanted nothing.
After so many years I've come back to meet
what's left, if anything is left,
of the city my ancestors loved
at the foot of this mountain.
In the foliage overhead, I listen to a golden rustling
the afternoon piles up.
Soon it will be cold.
May the Ávila save me.

Canto Lacrado

No pude separar el pájaro del canto.
Oí murmullos, ráfagas, acordes,
gotas de oráculo amarillo,
cosas indescifrables;
anoté cuanto pude sin espantarlo.
Me detuve abstraído ante sus ecos
sin indagar si modulaba un son antiguo
o si su voz se contamina
en esta hora llena de máquinas.
Lo oí después, lo seguí oyendo muchos días,
otro o el mismo, ya no supe, un canto
lacrado entre los pliegues de los aires.
Ignoro aún si trasmutaba en su inocencia
ruidos de goznes, pernos, hélices,
el zumbido de los taxis que van y vienen.
Ignoro si inventaba o traducía.
Sólo anoté una raya de su sombra
sin apartarla de sus alas.

Hidden Song

I couldn't distinguish the bird from the song.
I heard whispers, sudden blasts, chords,
golden oracles in droplets,
indecipherable things.
I jotted down as much as I could without startling it.
Absent-mindedly I stopped before its echoes
without worrying if it was modulating ancient sound
or if its voice was already contaminated
by this hour filled with machines.
I heard it later, I kept hearing it for many days,
another bird or the same, I didn't know,
a song hidden among the folds of the air.
I didn't even know if in its innocence
it was playing variations
on the sounds of hinges, bolts, screws,
the buzz of taxis as they come and go.
I don't know if it was inventing or translating.
I just got down one line of its shadow
without separating it from the wings.

Opus Número Cero

No sé qué calle iba a cruzar ahora,
ni con quién, cerca o lejos, pero es tarde.
Seguí los pasos de mi sombra, casi oyéndola,
entre las piedras del camino. Y se hizo tarde.
Y ni siquiera sé por qué ya es tarde...
No tarde de unos días o de unas noches,
sino del largo milenio en su crepúsculo,
del fin de siglo al que he venido y no era éste.

De pronto, me hallé a destiempo de mí mismo,
sentí la tierra gravitando a la deriva;
algo más que silencio faltaba en la palabra,
algo en el hombre que no es su vida ni su muerte.
Me vi sin horas para seguir mi estrella arcaica,
para alcanzar la flor que Dios no premedita.
Se me hizo tarde en este mundo y en el otro,
tarde en la niebla, los árboles, el viento.
Iba a anunciar un gallo el nuevo siglo
y sin que oyéramos su grito ya era póstumo.
Mi tiempo se cernía sobre un piano sin teclas,
opus número cero, sonando para nadie.

Opus Number Zero

I don't know what street I'm going to cross now
nor with whom, near or far, but it's late.
I followed my shadow's footsteps, almost heard it
on the road's cobblestones. And it was late.
And I don't even know why it's so late . . .
Not late by a few days or a few nights,
but by the long millennium in its twilight,
by the century's end to which I've come, and it's not even that.

Suddenly I was out of time with myself,
I felt the earth breaking adrift,
something more than silence lost from speech,
something missing from man
that's not his life or his death.
With no hours left to follow my outdated star,
to reach the flower God never planned,
it was getting late for me in this world and in the other,
late amid fog, trees, wind.
A cock would soon announce the new century;
we will hear nothing, but its cry is already posthumous.
For me time stands poised over a piano without keys,
opus number zero, playing for no one.

Una Fotografía de 1948

Amarillos maizales de la casa
frontera al río de enormes piedras.
Blasina adolescente con dos amigas
cuyos nombres olvido. ¡Cuántos verdores
y ebrios aromas de espesos yerbazales!...
Mi ceño ostenta el tácito reproche
de quien desdeña aquel país agrario
que no termina de enterrar a Gómez.
Entre la puerta y el camino
median tres cuadras rectas y arboladas.
De pronto un *click* me borra cincuenta años.
Ya Blasina no finge entre mohínes
morderse los cabellos
y del denso maizal nadie retiene
un solo grano.
Queda el mismo país siempre soleado,
de feraces paisajes, veloz música,
minas, planicies y petróleo,
país de amada sangre en nuestras venas,
que no termina de enterrar a Gómez.

A Photograph from 1948

Yellow cornfields of the house
facing a river of enormous stones.
Blasina an adolescent with two friends
whose names I forget. So many green fields,
all those intoxicating scents of herb gardens! . . .
My frown betrays the silent reproach
of someone who disdains this agrarian country
that's never managed to bury Gómez.
From the house to the road
an acre and a half of shady trees.
Suddenly a *click* wipes out fifty years.
Now Blasina no longer pulls faces
and pretends to bite her hair;
of the dense cornfield
no one has kept a single grain.
The same sun-washed countryside remains,
untamed landscapes, fast music,
mines, wide plains, petroleum,
this land of of ours flowing in our veins
that's never managed to bury Gómez.

Partitura de la Cigarra

XV

Y miré mi ciudad, mi bosque pétreo,
alto en la torre del árbol donde vivo,
alto en el bosque de edificios blancos...
Yo y mis ojos de palo,
yo y la sonora cigarra de mi sangre
con el geórgico canto que estos soles
me habituaron a oír desde hace tantos años.

Estuve oyendo el tiempo que pasa con su música,
el tiempo con sus vueltas de ayer y de mañana,
el tiempo redondo que nos trae y nos lleva
según la variación de su cantata.
Y oí mi vida en su pregón insomne
cuando en sus sones regresan mis mayores
no sé de dónde, hacia este bosque de edificios,
pese a los años que me separan de sus pasos,
aunque no sepa ahora cómo verlos
y se me vuelvan un liviano murmullo
que se prolonga a lo largo del patio.

Yo y el misterio de sus voces en la mía
ante un postigo de esta torre sin nadie,
yo y los sonidos que nos escoltan por el mundo,
el sonido de la tierra que gira,
el sonido del cuerpo que crepita en su llama,
el sonido de la cigarra cuya ignota partitura
avienta su clamor en nuestros campos.

The Cicada's Score

XV

And I looked at my city, my stone forest,
high in the tower of the tree where I live,
high in the forest of white buildings . . .
I and my eyes of pale straw,
I and the sonorous cicada of my blood
with its earth-bound song I'm so used to hearing
under this familiar sun so many years.

I was listening to the music of time passing,
time with its changes of yesterday and tomorrow,
the roundness of time that drags us and lifts us
through all the variations of its cantata.
I hear the sleepless prayer of my life
as my ancestors return in its sounds,
I don't know from where, to this forest of buildings.
The years divide me from their footsteps,
and nowdays I wouldn't know how to see them.
All they would be
is a pale murmuring going on and on
down the patio.

I with the strangeness of their voices trapped inside my voice
standing by the entranceway to this tower with no inhabitants,
I with the sounds hidden from us in this world,
the sound the earth makes as it spins,
the sound of the body crackling in its flames,
the cicada's sound – the cicada with its unknown score
raising a din in our fields.

Miré despacio mi vasto bosque pétreo,
yo que a veces escribo una forma de canto,
un poema sin élitros,
algún hexámetro sin alas.
Miré las sombras que pueblan las calles,
las absortas estatuas bajo la lluvia,
el recto espacio donde brota la música
que prodiga sus ecos en la cigarra.

Y aunque en el aire miré mi propia ausencia,
cuando mis huesos retornen al silencio
y se extinga la lumbre de esta lámpara,
sé que mañana habrá otras voces en la tierra,
ellas y el grito inmóvil o variable,
ellas y lo que no sabemos de nosotros,
lo que nadie descifra en una vida,
aunque se integre al hechizado coro
según su milagrosa partitura
la cigarra que sueña en nuestra sangre.

Slowly I looked out at my vast stone forest,
I who sometimes write a type of song,
a poem with no wing-sheafs,
some flightless hexameter.
I looked at the shadows that crowd its streets,
statue-like figures lost in concentration under the rain,
the narrow space where music breaks forth
lavishing its echoes on the cicada.

Though I saw my own absence in the air around me
as my bones return to silence,
as the light by which I write goes out,
I know tomorrow there will be other voices on earth,
other voices and the one constant cry with variations,
other voices and what we don't know of ourselves,
what no one deciphers in a lifetime,
even if the cicada dreaming in our blood
follows its miraculous score to the end,
becomes a note made whole
in the magician's choir.

Selected Prose Writings

The White Workshop

Nowdays, anyone who feels drawn towards an apprenticeship in poetry, despite the many impediments which might dissuade them from it, whether for good or ill, can finally embark on their vocation by means of a poetry workshop. The experiment is something new among us but, as in many other cases, it can count on a large number of defenders and detractors. Though operating in more or less identical form (i.e. the gathering together of a guide and a select dozen participants) poetry workshops can produce results as disparate as the groups of people they are made of. Much depends on the backgrounds and sensitivies of the participants, and above all, the fraternal cordial climate which can begin to develop through practice. That from the start each can distinguish their own voice in the chorus, that everyone sees the guide as persuasive interlocutor rather than hegemonic dictator, is doubtless a good point of departure. The habit of fertile discussion, the stimulus to work, mutual respect and everything which, to use an expression of Matthew Arnold's, we could call "literary urbanity", follow naturally from such a beginning.

For my part I don't underestimate the usefulness of workshops, although I secretly feel sceptical about their results. I nourish the prejudice (somewhat romantic it's true) that poetry like every art is a solitary passion. A multitude, as Simone Weil wisely advises, cannot even add up; a person needs to withdraw into solitude to execute this simple operation. For this reason maybe the title given by Schoenberg to his Memoirs strikes me as one of the most appropriate to sum up the meanderings of a life devoted to art, to any art: *How to regain solitude.* Only in isolation do we succeed in glimpsing the part of ourselves which is intransferrible, and maybe, paradoxically, that is the only part worth communicating to others.

I know that many would reply that in poetry, apart from innate gifts, there is the side of workmanship, strictly technical, common to other arts as to the modest labour of goldsmiths and handcraft makers. These are the so-called secrets of the trade, whose mastery is to a certain extent communicable. On the other hand, there are those who would remind me of Lautréamont's well-known aphorism: poetry should be made by all. The vast body of folklore seems to confirm the triumph of such multiple anonymous contributions. In this process, words become polished by rolling back and forth between people, like stones in a river, and the ones which endure turn out in the end to be the ones most valued by the collective soul. All that is true, with the proviso that we don't forget that at every instant there existed a real person, that they were never mere teams, however numerous we believe these makers to be. Yes, poetry should be made by all, but fatally written by one alone.

On the other hand, as far as there is a correspondence between poetry and an artisan's methods of working, the secrets of the trade, that vast area which R.G. Collingwood analyses in his book *The principles of art* , it seems to me that it is to this field that people in a workshop can really usefully devote themselves. Given that we write in our own language, it is in this, principally, (i.e. through the creations which make up its tradition) that we can investigate the how of its intimate government; of the why and the when we can usefully learn not only in our own language but in however many other languages we master.

The word "workshop", according to the Dictionary of the Spanish Royal Academy, has two accepted meanings, one concrete, the other figurative. The first refers to a place where an item of handwork is produced. The second refers to a school or scientific seminar where many people come together for common learning. The poetry workshop means both the first and the second. It is a workshop in both the literal and the figurative sense. There is an item of handwork as well as participation in a common apprenticeship. I, and those more or less of my age, never knew poetry workshops such as they exist today. We never had the fortune or misfortune of gathering together to initiate ourselves into the trade of poetry. Where, then, did we go to learn it? Others would reply, of course, with their personal stories of beginnings and influences. Personally, I have stated that I never assisted in any place where I gained the experience of this trade. That at least, because I believed it, is what I have repeated. I would like now to rectify this vain assertion. When I was a child, very much a child, I was intensely involved in one such place. I spent a lot of time in the white workshop.

It was a real workshop, just as it really was our daily bread. As a boy my father had learnt the trade of baker. He began, like any apprentice, sweeping up and lifting crates, and with the years he succeeded in becoming *maestro de cuadra*. Later he owned his own bakery, the workshop where I spent a large part of my infancy. I don't know how I could have previously overlooked what I owe for my art and my life to that room, to those men who ritually night after night would gather before the large tables to make bread. I am talking of an old bakery, the kind that doesn't exist now, in a large house big enough to pile up wood, to store hundreds of sacks of flour and to place in position the straight trays where the massed dough slowly gained body during the night in front of the oven. These are ancient, almost medieval proceedings, slower and more complicated than those of today, but also more filled with mythic presences. The sense of progress has reduced this workshop to a small cubicle of electrical appliances where the task is simplified by mechanical means. Now there is no need for cartloads of wood with its penetrating resinous fragrance, nor is there flour piled up in numerous store rooms. Why? The oven instead of being a yawning chamber of red-hot bricks is now a high-voltage metallic rectangle. I wonder, could a boy of today learn something for his poetry in that enwalled pigsty? I don't know. In the white workshop perhaps stayed fixed for me one of those mythic ambiences that Bachelard recreated to analyse *the poetry of space*. Flour is the essential substance which stores those years in my memory. Its whiteness contaminated everything: the fringe of your hair, the hands, the skin, but also things, gestures, words. Our house stood there like an igloo, the dwelling of an eskimo, under dense snow. For that reason, when years later in Paris for the first time I contemplated the quiet fall of snow, I didn't show the usual amazement of a man of the tropics. That old friend was already known to me. I felt only a vague curiosity to verify by touch its smooth presence.

I am speaking of a real poetic apprenticeship, of techniques I still use in my nights of work, for I don't want to weave metaphors around a simple memory. This very thing I'm saying, my nights, comes from there. The task of the bread makers was nocturnal like mine, accustomed to the late peaceful hours which make up for the oppressive heat of a midsummer day. Like them I've got used to the strangeness of the laborious vigil while around us everyone is asleep. And in the depths of night whiteness is doubly white. The moon is present on the walls, the wood, the tables, the caps of the workers. The learned and wise workers. There is the air of an operating theatre, the silent steps, the quick movements. It is no less than bread what is silently being made here, the bread they will ask for at dawn to take to hospitals, colleges, barracks, houses. What labour can share so much responsibility? Isn't it the same preoccupation as poetry?

The oven, which purifies all that, reddens whoever works there with its invigorating fire. Loaves of dough, once formed into a mass, are covered with a cloth and placed in large bowls like sleeping fish, until the moment comes when they are ready to be baked. How often, setting aside the first draft of a poem to revise it sometime later, I've felt I'm covering it myself with a cloth to decide its fate later on. And I have said nothing of those labourers, serene, serious, and tough, with their mythology of slums, of cheap liquor. Should I seek for the sacred further off in my life, paint human purity with a different face? Christ could change stones into bread, for that reason he was more like a carpenter, that beautiful workshop with its distinctive colour. For those men who never spoke to me of religion, perhaps because they were too religious, Christ was in the humility of flour and the redness of the fire that started burning at midnight.

From the white workshop I gained the sense of devotion to existence which I found so often in those masters of the nocturnal. The care due to the making of things, the brotherhood which is part of a common destiny, the search for a friendly wisdom which doesn't lead us to lie to ourselves too much. How many times, looking at the books lined up before me, I've thought of the line of trays filled with bread. Can a word reach a page with more care, with more intimate attention than that given by those workers to what they produced? I would give anything sometimes to approximate to the perfect execution of their nightly workshops. To the white workshop I owe these and many other teachings which I value when I face the writing of a text.

Bread and words join in my imagination, made sacred by the same persistence. By night, sitting down in front of the empty page, I see in my lamp a halo of that ancient whiteness which has never abandoned me. I no longer see the bakers, it's true, nor hear close by their fraternal chatter; instead of burning wood shining strips of neon surround me; the song of roosters is replaced by wailing sirens and the sound of taxis. The fury of the modern city has driven far away the things and the time of the white workshop. And yet the ritual of its nights survives in me. In each word I write, I feel the prolongation of the watch that gathered those humble artisans together.

Maybe if I had not been involved in its daily watches, if I had not been mixed up in the deep ceremonies of its labours, I would in any case have found something that fed my desire for poetry. The cry of Merlin would have always tempted me to follow its trail in the forest. Nevertheless, I can't imagine where, if not there, I would have learned my word to recognise the sacred devotion of life. I jot down this last line and listen to the crackling of the wood, I watch the cloud of smoke spreading, the iconic faces coming and going through the room, the flour meticulously covering the memory of the white workshop.

from the collection of essays *El Taller Blanco*,
Mexico, 1996

Fragments

"The crime against life," Archibald MacLeish said, "the worst of all crimes, is not to feel." Not to feel the world, not to feel life in its numerous mysteries, in the constant simplicity it shows, forms in truth a deeply serious mutilation. Nevertheless, it's important not only to feel but to learn to feel, to learn to define the boundary between true feeling and simple arousal of emotion which is its most common and spurious substitute. "In the fully emotional man," W.B. Yeats tells us his father advised him, "the least awakening of feeling forms a harmony in which every chord of every feeling vibrates. Excitation is by itself of an insufficiently emotive nature, the common vibration of one or two chords alone."

To learn to feel: this task alone, which is nothing small, would do more to form a young poet than all the apprenticeship devoted to knowledge of literature, rules, fashions, etc. The manuals frequently forget this essential fact, without which every creative attempt is useless. Through feeling you can validly conquer the language which expresses it; feeling itself, when it is legitimate, creates its own form or the possibility of inventing it. The opposite, in contrast, is less probable. How to get down from the web of formalities to the emotional nakedness of the world?

~

In all true art you can see, as an extraordinary gift, a certain principle of concatenation, that is a certain interdependence of one element with another, a single identical thread which lets us suppose – and all Platonism does no more than suspect this – that the author is only a medium, a momentary agent of revelation. Whether this is explained along romantic lines or not, the principle enables us validly to measure the greatness of a work and its absolute dependence on an inner necessity. A portrait by Rembrandt, for example, always possesses this attractive uniqueness as does a poem by Blake or Verlaine. By detecting the union of elements that flow from a profound necessary concatenation (which certainly is profound because it's not enough to wish for it to make it appear in a work) as can be seen in so many present day texts, we are in a position to understand what separates mere trickery or expertise from superior art.

~

We can't demand that today's painters believe in God or some form of divinity because no one can demand that of another, despite the fury of converts. But we can suggest to them that they try to paint the world as previously those with a religious vocation might have done. Only in this way can they escape a little from the sad dictates of the artistic marketplace.

~

Juan Ramón Jiménez used to dedicate his work "to the immense minority". Years later, poets of opposite tastes, though not always with the Andalusian's talent, dedicated theirs "to the immense majority". As poets of our own time, with less talent than all these, we work for the immense majority, for the immense minority, and finally for whoever comes or goes.

~

The criticism made of "verse measured by the metronome", reiterated in our time by Pound, has been repeated so often you could say it has made a fortune. Perhaps to defend himself against it, Eliot stated that no verse is truly free, that there are only "good lines, bad lines and chaos". Despite this he adds elsewhere that he never wrote with attention to the scansion of a line, which doesn't mean he censured such practices in a fanatical way. Nevertheless, Pound's assertion doesn't in any way cancel the difference in tone that two poets can successfully bring to the one metre, cutting their verse to the same metronome. How different is the hendecasyllable of Quevedo from that of Bécquer, for example! In both there is tension but the tone is misty and enveloping in Bécquer, pared down and lineal in Quevedo. There is metronome in the art of all the classics and anyone may learn to use it appropriately if they are secretly interested, but the gift of transcending the metronome, of conquering a distinctive valid tone, seems reserved for very few.

〜

Reading the moving letters of John Keats you can see an alliance of innocence and knowledge – in the sense that he reserved for that word – similar to the echo of Hölderlin, and fatally distant now from our own days. I'm not referring to what his art succeeds in telling us, which I believe is close to the soul of all time, given that his greatness makes it timeless, but to the sense of "earthly innocence" which makes it possible and which has vanished forever from us. The modern poet is tough, as Friedrich observes; he lashes out or makes jokes, begs or turns ironic, maybe because he knows he is separated from that innocent purity. It's something not easy to define, but which we see corroborated in the art of our time; maybe for that reason poetry has become more and more solitary. This idea could well be illustrated through statements of Ungaretti ("I seek a country of innocence", "poetry is a thirst for insatiable innocence") – maybe the last great poet to center his work from this perspective . . . How distant from him appears Montale, his fellow countryman, for example. The press, the contemporary means of mass communication, seem to presuppose a pact of language, which we can accept or reject, but which it is not possible for us to avoid, unless we are a child, a madman, an "innocent".

〜

Before the poem which is strictly ours we are weak. Supreme force resides within it. What the poem demands is weakness to invade, therefore the power of reason is almost always an obstacle to it. The authentic poet learns to dismantle the resistance (not to arm it, as the literary manuals advise); he creates mechanisms and reflexes of defencelessness so that the poem may invade him. In this way then, creation is passively feminine, and the more passive, the more deeply it contributes to giving birth to the poetic voice.

~

Many poems anticipate their first sigh on our lips. They rise towards us out of living depths, but then die suddenly, suffocated by a form that doesn't suit them. The intuition of form is as necessary as the initial breath itself which gives them life. Maybe, when doubt overtakes our first attempts, the best thing is to sketch out a treatment from a variety of formal directions till the right measure is found.

~

Dreams comfort us because they reveal the certainty, half lost, that while something dreams in us, the true poetic faculty remains intact. And it isn't that dreams directly supply poetry, but one and the other, as we know, drink at the same fountain.

~

When foreign poetic trends and forms are followed very closely, as seems to happen now with so many creators in our language, we mustn't forget that, by using our language, what is achieved will differ substantially, just as the respective linguistic structures and the rhythm of everyday speech differ. It is the same as what happens with exquisite recipes from another's kitchen. In the end it's no use knowing the recipes, memorising proportions and procedures, when the moment we start cooking we can only rely on the ingredients we find everyday in our own markets. Invention which disdains what is our own, what we have lying ready to hand, runs the risk of becoming arbitrary and insipid.

~

The extraordinary sensation of drawing close to a poem as to a village which, from far off, can be made out in the fog. Brief points of light start to become rectangles till they identify themselves for us as windows. Straight pools of background clarity – these are the stanzas. It's a pleasure to look at them close up and guess what is there, under the lamp of each rectangle. It's an even greater pleasure from far off to wonder what each thing will be like there, which of the various shapes we think we see will be the true one, if it is really a village where we are going, if we're not just wandering about lost.

~

One of the most common inconveniences we poets face nowdays is successfully to forge an art which does without God, employing an essentially Catholic sensibility. In each of us, even at a very advanced age, survive the more or less neglected rituals of creole Catholicism, the household altars, in short the whole series of practices brought from Europe and adapted to the tropics. A simple outward declaration is not enough to free us from practices which have shaped our way of feeling and judging. And in poetry, which above all is the expression of our deepest truths, the contradiction appears more often than we suspect. Doubtless it is an advantage if the poet recognises the problem early and, without violating the maturity of his conscience, opens up and celebrates with the common people the rituals and religious sentiments belonging to the place where he was born. So Manuel Bandeira, for example, can appropriately use the name of the Virgin Mary because, without being at all a believer, he sees in her a humble Brazilian mother or, at least, a glimpse of what that Brazilian mother feels devoted to. The problem becomes more poignant and paradoxical in Murilo Mendes, another Brazilian. Recognisably Catholic, Mendes often gives expression to a pagan erotic world, thereby (perhaps unconsciously) adding much tension to his writing. It could be said that in Mendes two religions survive, often with hostlility, yet with humour and balanced graciousness.

~

Maybe not the greatest advice – what could be that? – but one that frequently comes back into my mind consists of a biographic detail of Paul Klee. From what is said, shortly before travelling to Italy he went though a deep adolescent crisis, recognising that he had equal abilities for poetry, painting and music, without being able to decide to which of them he should devote himself. It was then that he said to himself: first of all succeed in being a man. Everything else will follow clearly from that.

∾

What sometimes irritates in T. S. Eliot is that he almost always inserts quotations from poets of the past in his verses, while he completely omits quotations from poets of the future.

∾

There are poems that seem like an interrupted chess game where the author has meditated very carefully beforehand and left us his final sealed move. We read them not to enjoy a particular pleasure – that too has become old fashioned – but to wonder where the checkmate will come from.

∾

The poet tries to read God in his original language, convinced from birth that the foreign translations are of little use.

∾

The unavoidable theme, today's true poetic fact is the absurd possibility of atomic devastation, a possibility whose real threat is inseparable from every sensation and every thought. Man, any half-awake man, in our days suffers the terror of this risk, and the poet more than any, given that since antiquity he has fulfilled the role of lightning conductor. Nevertheless, it's not necessary for every line to refer to the possible extermination that approaches all of us. It's enough to recognise that in every object that forms the motive of the poet's attention, the catastrophic ingredient is implicit to a degree completely unknown to artists of other epochs. Looked at this way, the apocalyptic notion has now become an extraordinary element of our modernity.

~

Jean Cocteau's preoccupation with once more invoking the rose against miserable reproductions of *the flowers of evil* deserves some attention, above all when these flowers now come to us from the hands of gardeners less expert than those of last century. All the same no one knows what rose our epoch demands because, despite Gertrude Stein, not all roses are the same.

~

In all the words of a poem you must be able to read their necessity, that is one by one they should convince us that they are there because they are more necessary than other words which were not used, and, what is even more complicated, that they are more valid than silence itself. ("In art it is difficult to say something which would be as good as saying nothing", affirmed Wittgenstein.) Necessity constitutes the principle guide of the poet; nothing helps as much as feeling to clarify what is truly necessary.

~

A large part of present day lyric poetry has sacrificed the musical principle of other epochs without doing the hard work of substituting some other equivalent for it. They rely more on the idea and disdain the music, condemning us to the production of an intellectual masculine art. By proceeding this way, it has been forgotten that poetry should create a music that makes us think.

~

Maybe we pay too much attention to lyric virtuosity, especially to a certain mental virtuosity. And the worst thing is, as Cocteau warns, that all virtuosity fatally leads to banality.

≈

The poet has in common with the spider the art of creating form. Other animals also work in this way, like birds making their nest or bees in their hive, but with the poet as with the spider the form is secreted without outside help, in total solitude. The symmetry with which the spider reproduces a certain innate order is the basis for the survival of its species, as also in the poet language establishes a certain symmetry, which forms a definitely vital element for the survival of all.

≈

Reading a poem my first curiosity consists in discovering the distance between the I of the speaker and the generic body of the words. It's a matter of an activity of verification which, through my habits as a reader, has become indispensable with the years. The distance I verify bears hardly any relation to the quality of the poetic text; almost always it is independent of that, and at most constitutes a stylish sketch, a manner of positioning yourself before the poem's individual space. Later a different related preoccupation works on me, that of knowing or discovering if that chosen distance is in the end fully justified in the total composition. (I think of Villon, the reprobate, speaking in the voice of his mother to Our Lady of Paris, an artificial distance doubtless, but thanks to his genius it becomes legitimate and convincing.) The rhythm, the tone, precision, and everything which contributes to the verbal accuracy of the lyric object, seem to me results of that distance, and, even more, results of the care taken to choose that distance as the most suitable at the time of ordering the poem's words.

≈

With a good poem we always know where each line is taking us. The moments of its writing appear fully realised. You can feel the power of the author and the speed with which he ties together the elements of his imagination. Even when the poem contains weaker, less successful areas, we manage to limit these and even excuse them, because it is always sufficiently clear what the poem intends. Less successful poets, on the other hand, only manage to get tangled up in a dull rhythm without letting us know where they want to go. In the end we prefer to abandon the reading before guessing their destination.

~

Feeling is fertile because only it deeply illuminates us. Invention/ cleverness distracts us, sharpens, polishes; it reaches the brain but not the soul. It enriches us with a false gold because it always leaves us with dangling stories. "Feeling is everything – said Goethe – man is sound and smoke."

~

The recommendation of T. S. Eliot that it is necessary to dedicate several hours a week to poetry through the whole of one's life is directed at the profession of poet, the artesanal, technical side, which, in every art, it is good to know and master. This is the common zone the poet, the painter and the musician share with patient artisans, as R. G. Collingwood lucidly analysed in his book *The principles of art*. But, as Collingwood tells us, by itself it is not art or poetry. You can dedicate more time than Eliot advised without the result necessarily being artistic. There is, then, this other margin, the zone of the daimon, of Lorca's *duende*, for whom there are no formulas. Touching on this other side, the wise Eliot, "monarchic, classic and anglican", perhaps would not have stopped thinking of Psalm 127, according to which, "every success depends on divine protection. It is vain for you to get up early, to go to bed late, and to eat the bread of pain; it is Yahweh who in dreams gives bread to his chosen."

~

The poem is a prayer spoken to a God who only exists while the prayer lasts.

from the collection of essays *El Taller Blanco*,
Mexico, 1996

Notes to the Poems

LOS ÁRBOLES / THE TREES: "Un tordo negro" – a black thrush. The bird called a "tordo" in Venezuela differs in colour from what is called a thrush in North America. It is black in colour. Though similar to a starling its beak and head have a different shape. I have generally translated the word as "thrush" but in one place, where its colour is vital to the poem, I have referred to it as "blackbird". ("Un canto para el tordo")

GÜIGÜE, 1918: Güigüe – a town in central Venezuela in the region of Valencia, where Montejo's father lived. This poem recalls the events surrounding the outbreak of the Spanish Influenza epidemic in 1918.

PARTIDA / DEPARTURE: Montejo travelled several times to Europe by boat. Travel and time spent abroad were an important part of Montejo's life. He lived in Paris 1968–1971, Buenos Aires 1978–79, and Lisbon 1988 to 1994.

DOS REMBRANDT / TWO REMBRANDTS: This poem refers to two self portraits by Rembrandt exhibited side by side in the Rijksmuseum, Amsterdam.

LISBOA / LISBON: Montejo was Venezuela's cultural attaché in Lisbon from 1988 to 1994 and was captivated by the beauty of the city.

NOCHES DE TRANSATLÁNTICO / NIGHTS ON THE TRANSATLANTIC: A homage to the French poet Jules Supervielle who was born in Uruguay and spent much of his life travelling by boat between Montevideo and France. Supervielle lost both his parents in infancy. Montejo's collection of poetry *Terredad* carries an epigraph from Supervielle: *C'était le temps inoubliable où nous étions sur la terre.*

MANOA: The legendary city of gold long sought by the Conquistadors. Sir Walter Raleigh was one of those who tried to find this mythic city, the capital of El Dorado. His book, first published in London in 1596, entitled in its Spanish translation "El descubrimiento del extenso, rico y bello Imperio de Guayana, y la relación de la grande y dorada ciudad de Manoa", was a best seller of the 16th century.

UN TORDO / A THRUSH: Line 5–6: The term "tertuliantes" –from the word "Tertulia", a meeting of people who gather to amuse themselves through conversation. Lacking a simple English equivalent, I chose "chattering intelligentsia" as a concise phrase that fitted the context, though it adds a negative feel not really there in the Spanish.

ADIÓS A MI PADRE / SAYING GOODBYE TO MY FATHER: "'Apamate' is the name of one of our most beautiful trees. It's a Venezuelan word, very everyday here. It is probable – as happens with other terms for tropical flora – that this tree has a different name in other countries in Central or South America. It's a tree which in the month of May loses all its leaves and stays for several days completely filled with flowers. Their colour varies from intense lilac to pale rose to the purest white. If the Chinese had this tree they would plant groves of it and hold festivals on the days when it is in flower." (E.M. in correspondence, responding to translator's query – translation P.B)

FINAL DE LLUVIA / AFTER THE RAIN: 3rd stanza last line: "donde rondan amores bisiestos". "Bisiestos", literally leap-year, is an unusual usage here coined by Montejo after a Brazilian poet's use of the Portuguese equivalent to refer to poets who wrote only once in a "blue moon", then gathered their poems after ten years or so to publish in anthologies. "Laziest of lovers" seemed to cover the essential idea, while keeping the brevity.

AL RETORNO / COMING BACK: the Ávila – the mountain that overlooks Caracas.

UNA FOTOGRAFÍA DE 1948 / A PHOTOGRAPH FROM 1948: The poem describes the former house of the poet's father, Eduardo, a farmhouse commonly called a *finca* in Spanish America, on the outskirts of Maracay City. The house and land have since vanished into urban development. Juan Vicente Gómez was the dictator of Venezuela from 1908 to 1935. See Miguel Gomes' Introduction for a discussion of this poem.

Bibliography

1. Books of Poetry by Eugenio Montejo (in Spanish)

Élegos. Caracas: Editorial Arte, 1967.
Muerte y memoria. Caracas: U.C., 1972.
Algunas palabras. Caracas: Monte Ávila Editores, 1976.
Terredad. Caracas: Monte Ávila Editores, 1978.
Trópico absoluto. Caracas: Fundarte, 1982.
Alfabeto del mundo. A. Ferrari, prologue. Barcelona: Laia, 1987 [This
    volume is the first edition of the book named after its title
    poem. It also includes a selection from all of Montejo's
    previous books. In 1988, under the same title, the F.C.E. of
    Mexico published another, very extensive compilation of the
    author's work].
[Sergio Sandoval, heteronym]. *Guitarra del horizonte.* Caracas: Alfadil,
    1991.
[Tomás Linden, heteronym]. *El hacha de seda.* Caracas: Goliardos, 1995.
Antología. [Includes the unpublished *Nostalgia de Bolívar,* 1976, as well
    as a wide selection from all his previous books]. F. J. Cruz Pérez,
    pról. Caracas: Monte Ávila Editores, 1996.
El azul de la tierra (antología poética). [Includes selections of the
    heteronym Tomás Linden]. Bogotá: Norma, 1997.
Adiós al siglo XX. Sevilla: Renacimiento, 1997 [a less extensive
    preliminary version of this book first appeared in Lisbon,
    1992].
Partitura de la cigarra. Madrid/Buenos Aires/Valencia: Pre-Textos, 1999.
Tiempo Transfigurado. Valencia, Ven.: Universidad de Carabobo, 2001
Papiros amorosos. Madrid: Pre-Textos, 2002. Second edition with
    additional poems, Fundación Bigott, Caracas, 2003.

2. Books of Essays

La ventana oblicua. Valencia, Ven.: Universidad de Carabobo, 1974.

[Blas Coll, heteronym]. *El cuaderno de Blas Coll*. 1981. Caracas: Alfadil,
    1983 [corrected and extended edition].
El taller blanco. Caracas: Fundarte, 1983 [also in an extended edition
    with new essays – México: UAM, 1996].

3. POETRY AVAILABLE IN ENGLISH TRANSLATION

Alastair Reid – translations of the poems "Dos cuerpos", "Algunas
    palabras", "La Vida", "Al fin de todo" , "El Orinoco" and "En
    esta ciudad" in *Translation* (The journal of literary translations),
    Volume XXIX, Spring 1994, Columbia University, New York.

4. CRITICISM (IN SPANISH)

Cruz Pérez, Francisco José. "Eugenio Montejo: el viaje total" in
    Eugenio Montejo, *Antología*: 7–25.
Eyzaguirre, Luis. "Eugenio Montejo: poesía de fin de siglo" in Julio
    Ortega, ed. *Venezuela: fin de siglo*. Caracas: La Casa de Bello, 1993:
    213–222.
Ferrari, Américo. "Eugenio Montejo y el alfabeto del mundo" in
    Eugenio Montejo, *Alfabeto del mundo*: 5–28.
Figueredo, Juan Medina. *La terredad de Orfeo: tensión constructiva del
    habla en la poesía de Eugenio Montejo*. Valencia, Venezuela:
    Gobierno de Carabobo, 1997.
Gomes, Miguel. "Naturaleza e historia en la poesía de Eugenio
    Montejo". *Revista Iberoamericana* 201 (2002): 1005–1024.
—— "Poesía de la estación perdida: tres aproximaciones a la lírica de
    Eugenio Montejo". *El pozo de las palabras*. Caracas: Fundarte,
    1990: 99–123.
—— *Poéticas del ensayo venezolano del siglo XX*. Cranston, Rhode Island:
    Ediciones Inti, 1996: 205–210.

——— "Postvanguardia y heteronimia en la poesía de Eugenio Montejo". *Hispanic Journal* 19-1 (1998): 9-22.

Gutiérrez Plaza, Arturo. "El alfabeto de la terredad: estudio de la poética en la obra de Eugenio Montejo". *Revista Iberoamericana* 166-7 (1994): 549-60.

Hernández, Consuelo. "La arquitectura poética de Eugenio Montejo" in Julio Ortega, ed. *Venezuela: fin de siglo*. Caracas: La Casa de Bello, 1993: 223-233.

Lastra, Pedro. "El pan y las palabras: poesía de Eugenio Montejo" in Pedro Lastra y Luis Eyzaguirre, eds. *Catorce poetas hispanoamericanos de hoy*. Número monográfico de la revista Inti. Rhode Island. 18-9 (1984): 211-215.

López Parada, Esperanza. "La palabra en su sentido primero". ABC Cultural. Madrid.(22/1/2000): 11.

Rivera, Francisco. "El cuaderno de Blas Coll". *Ulises y el laberinto*. Caracas: Fundarte, 1983: 71-87.

——— "La poesía de Eugenio Montejo". *Inscripciones*. Caracas: Fundarte, 1982: 87-110. [Also available in Francisco Rivera. *Entre el silencio y la palabra*. Caracas: Monte Ávila, 1986: 39-58].

Sucre, Guillermo. *La máscara, la transparencia*. 1975. México: F.C.E., 1986: 309-12.

Printed in the United Kingdom
by Lightning Source UK Ltd.
101619UKS00001B/412-414